Sir Henry John Newbolt, Isaac Foot

The Island Race

Sir Henry John Newbolt, Isaac Foot

The Island Race

ISBN/EAN: 9783744732147

Printed in Europe, USA, Canada, Australia, Japan

Cover: Foto ©ninafisch / pixelio.de

More available books at **www.hansebooks.com**

THE ISLAND RACE

THE ISLAND RACE

BY

HENRY NEWBOLT

LONDON
ELKIN MATHEWS, VIGO STREET
1898

Copyright in America
All Rights Reserved

TO
ROBERT BRIDGES

Of the forty pieces in this volume, twelve were published in 1897 under the title of "Admirals All." Of the remaining twenty-eight many have appeared in the periodicals enumerated below: none were written earlier than "Admirals All." The thanks of the Author for permission to reprint are due to the Editors of *Longman's Magazine*, the *Spectator*, the *Daily Chronicle*, the *St. James's Gazette*, the *Saturday Review*, the *Pall Mall Magazine*, the *Windsor Magazine*, the *Pall Mall Gazette*, the *Speaker*, the *Outlook*, and the *Athenæum*.

Contents

	PAGE
The Vigil	1
Admiral Death	4
The Quarter Gunner's Yarn	7
For a Trafalgar Cenotaph	12
Craven	13
Messmates	16
The Death of Admiral Blake	18
Væ Victis	21
Minora Sidera	25
Laudabunt Alii	27
San Stefano	30

CONTENTS

	PAGE
Hawke	34
The Fighting Téméraire	36
Drake's Drum	40
Admirals All	42
Gillespie	46
Seringapatam	50
A Ballad of John Nicholson	55
The Guides at Cabul, 1879	61
The Gay Gordons	65
He Fell Among Thieves	67
Ionicus	71
The Non-Combatant	73
Clifton Chapel	75
England	78
The Echo	79
Vitaï Lampada	81
A Song of Exmoor	83
Fidele's Grassy Tomb	87
Gavotte	92
Imogen	94
Nel Mezzo del Cammin	96

CONTENTS

The Invasion	97
Pereunt et Imputantur	100
Felix Antonius	102
The Last Word	104
Ireland, Ireland	108
Moonset	109
Hymn	111
The Building of the Temple	113
Notes	118

O STRENGTH DIVINE OF ROMAN DAYS,
  O SPIRIT OF THE AGE OF FAITH,
GO WITH OUR SONS ON ALL THEIR WAYS,
  WHEN WE LONG SINCE ARE DUST AND WRAITH.

The Vigil

ENGLAND! where the sacred flame
  Burns before the inmost shrine,
Where the lips that love thy name
  Consecrate their hopes and thine,
Where the banners of thy dead
Weave their shadows overhead,
Watch beside thine arms to-night,
Pray that God defend the Right.

THE VIGIL

Think that when to-morrow comes
    War shall claim command of all,
Thou must hear the roll of drums,
    Thou must hear the trumpet's call.
Now, before they silence ruth,
Commune with the voice of truth;
England! on thy knees to-night
Pray that God defend the Right.

Hast thou counted up the cost,
    What to foeman, what to friend?
Glory sought is Honour lost,
    How should this be knighthood's end?
Know'st thou what is Hatred's meed?
What the surest gain of Greed?
England! wilt thou dare to-night
Pray that God defend the Right?

THE VIGIL

Single-hearted, unafraid,
    Hither all thy heroes came,
On this altar's steps were laid
    Gordon's life and Outram's fame.
England! if thy will be yet
By their great example set,
Here beside thine arms to-night
Pray that God defend the Right.

So shalt thou when morning comes
    Rise to conquer or to fall,
Joyful hear the rolling drums,
    Joyful hear the trumpets call.
Then let Memory tell thy heart;
"*England! what thou wert, thou art!*"
Gird thee with thine ancient might,
Forth! and God defend the Right!

Admiral Death

Boys, are ye calling a toast to-night?
  (Hear what the sea-wind saith)
Fill for a bumper strong and bright,
  And here's to Admiral Death!
He's sailed in a hundred builds o' boat,
He's fought in a thousand kinds o' coat,
He's the senior flag of all that float,
  And his name's Admiral Death.

ADMIRAL DEATH

Which of you looks for a service free?
  (Hear what the sea-wind saith)
The rules o' the service are but three
  When ye sail with Admiral Death.
Steady your hand in time o' squalls,
Stand to the last by him that falls,
And answer clear to the voice that calls,
  " Ay, Ay! Admiral Death!"

How will ye know him among the rest?
  (Hear what the sea-wind saith)
By the glint o' the stars that cover his breast
  Ye may find Admiral Death.
By the forehead grim with an ancient scar,
By the voice that rolls like thunder far,
By the tenderest eyes of all that are,
  Ye may know Admiral Death.

Where are the lads that sailed before?

(Hear what the sea-wind saith)

Their bones are white by many a shore,

They sleep with Admiral Death.

Oh! but they loved him, young and old,

For he left the laggard, and took the bold,

And the fight was fought, and the story's told,

And they sleep with Admiral Death.

The Quarter-Gunner's Yarn

We lay at St. Helen's, and easy she rode
With one anchor catted and freshwater stowed;
When the barge came alongside like bullocks we roared,
For we knew what we carried with Nelson aboard.

Our Captain was Hardy, the pride of us all,
I'll ask for none better when danger shall call,
He was hardy by nature and Hardy by name,
And soon by his conduct to honour he came.

The third day the Lizard was under our lee,
Where the Ajax and Thunderer joined us at sea,
But what with foul weather and tacking about,
When we sighted the Fleet we were thirteen days out.

The Captains they all came aboard quick enough,
But the news that they brought was as heavy as duff;
So backward an enemy never was seen,
They were harder to come at than Cheeks the Marine.

The lubbers had hare's lugs where seamen have ears,
So we stowed all saluting and smothered our cheers,
And to humour their stomachs and tempt them to dine
In the offing we showed them but six of the line.

One morning the topmen reported below
The old Agamemnon escaped from the foe;
Says Nelson " My lads, there'll be honour for some,
For we're sure of a battle now Berry has come."

"Up hammocks!" at last cried the bo'sun at dawn;
The guns were cast loose and the tompions drawn;
The gunner was bustling the shotracks to fill,
And "All hands to quarters" was piped with a will.

We now saw the enemy bearing ahead,
And to East of them Cape Traflagar it was said;
'Tis a name we remember from father to son,
That the days of old England may never be done.

The Victory led, to her flag it was due,
Tho' the Téméraires thought themselves Admirals too,
But Lord Nelson he hailed them with masterful grace,
"Cap'n Harvey, I'll thank you to keep in your place."

To begin with we closed the Bucentaure alone,
An eighty-gun ship, and their Admiral's own,
We raked her but once, and the rest of the day
Like a hospital hulk on the water she lay.

To our battering next the Redoubtable struck,
But her sharpshooters gave us the worst of the luck,
Lord Nelson was wounded most cruel to tell,
" They've done for me, Hardy," he cried as he fell.

To the cockpit in silence they carried him past,
And sad were the looks that were after him cast,
His face with a kerchief he tried to conceal,
But we knew him too well from the truck to the keel.

When the Captain reported a victory won,
" Thank God!" he kept saying, " my duty I've done."
At last came the moment to kiss him good-bye,
And the Captain for once had the salt in his eye.

" Now anchor, dear Hardy," the Admiral cried,
But before we could make it he fainted and died;
All night in the trough of the sea we were tossed,
And for want of groundtackle good prizes were lost.

Then we hauled down the flag, at the fore it was red,
And blue at the mizzen was hoisted instead
By Nelson's famed Captain, the pride of each tar,
Who fought in the Victory off Cape Traflagar.

For a Trafalgar Cenotaph

Lover of England, stand awhile and gaze
With thankful heart, and lips refrained from praise :
They rest beyond the speech of human pride
Who served with Nelson and with Nelson died.

Craven

(MOBILE BAY, 1864.)

OVER the turret, shut in his ironclad tower,
    Craven was conning his ship through smoke and flame;
Gun to gun he had battered the fort for an hour,
    Now was the time for a charge to end the game.

There lay the narrowing channel, smooth and grim,
    A hundred deaths beneath it, and never a sign;
There lay the enemy's ships, and sink or swim
    The flag was flying, and he was head of the line.

The fleet behind was jamming; the monitor hung
  Beating the stream; the roar for a moment hushed;
Craven spoke to the pilot; slow she swung;
  Again he spoke, and right for the foe she rushed.

Into the narrowing channel, between the shore
  And the sunk torpedoes lying in treacherous rank;
She turned but a yard too short; a muffled roar,
  A mountainous wave, and she rolled, righted, and sank.

Over the manhole, up in the ironclad tower,
  Pilot and Captain met as they turned to fly:
The hundredth part of a moment seemed an hour,
  For one could pass to be saved, and one must die.

They stood like men in a dream: Craven spoke,
  Spoke as he lived and fought, with a Captain's pride,
"After you, Pilot:" the pilot woke,
  Down the ladder he went, and Craven died.

All men praise the deed and the manner, but we—
  We set it apart from the pride that stoops to the proud,
The strength that is supple to serve the strong and free,
  The grace of the empty hands and promises loud:

Sidney thirsting a humbler need to slake,
  Nelson waiting his turn for the surgeon's hand,
Lucas crushed with chains for a comrade's sake,
  Outram coveting right before command,

These were paladins, these were Craven's peers,
  These with him shall be crowned in story and song,
Crowned with the glitter of steel and the glimmer of tears,
  Princes of courtesy, merciful, proud and strong.

Messmates

He gave us all a good-bye cheerily
   At the first dawn of day;
We dropped him down the side full drearily
   When the light died away.
It's a dead dark watch that he's a-keeping there,
And a long, long night that lags a-creeping there,
Where the Trades and the tides roll over him
   And the great ships go by.

He's there alone with green seas rocking him
   For a thousand miles round;
He's there alone with dumb things mocking him,
   And we're homeward bound.
It's a long, lone watch that he's a-keeping there,
And a dead cold night that lags a-creeping there,
While the months and the years roll over him
   And the great ships go by.

I wonder if the tramps come near enough
   As they thrash to and fro,
And the battle-ships bells ring clear enough
   To be heard down below;
If through all the lone watch that he's a-keeping there
And the long, cold night that lags a-creeping there
The voices of the sailor-men shall comfort him
   When the great ships go by.

The Death of Admiral Blake

(August 17th, 1657)

Laden with spoil of the South, fulfilled with the glory of achievement,
    And freshly crowned with never-dying fame,
Sweeping by shores where the names are the names of the victories of England,
    Across the Bay the squadron homeward came.

Proudly they came, but their pride was the pomp of a funeral at midnight,
    When dreader yet the lonely morrow looms;
Few are the words that are spoken, and faces are gaunt beneath the torchlight
    That does but darken more the nodding plumes.

Low on the field of his fame, past hope lay the Admiral triumphant,
    And fain to rest him after all his pain;
Yet for the love that he bore to his own land, ever unforgotten,
    He prayed to see the Western hills again.

Fainter than stars in a sky long gray with the coming of the daybreak,
    Or sounds of night that fade when night is done,
So in the death-dawn faded the splendour and loud renown of warfare,
    And life of all its longings kept but one.

"Oh! to be there for an hour when the shade draws in beside the hedgerows,
    And falling apples wake the drowsy noon:
Oh! for the hour when the elms grow sombre and human in the twilight,
    And gardens dream beneath the rising moon.

"Only to look once more on the land of the memories of childhood,

  Forgetting weary winds and barren foam :

Only to bid farewell to the combe and the orchard and the moorland,

  And sleep at last among the fields of home!"

So he was silently praying, till now, when his strength was ebbing faster,

  The Lizard lay before them faintly blue ;

Now on the gleaming horizon the white cliffs laughed along the coast-line,

  And now the forelands took the shapes they knew.

There lay the Sound and the Island with green leaves down beside the water,

  The town, the Hoe, the masts, with sunset fired—

Dreams!.ay, dreams of the dead! for the great heart faltered on the threshold,

  And darkness took the land his soul desired.

Væ Victis

Beside the placid sea that mirrored her
    With the old glory of dawn that cannot die,
The sleeping city began to moan and stir,
    As one that fain from an ill dream would fly;
    Yet more she feared the daylight bringing nigh
Such dreams as know not sunrise, soon or late,—
    Visions of honour lost and power gone by,
Of loyal valour betrayed by factious hate,
And craven sloth that shrank from the labour of forging fate.

They knew and knew not, this bewildered crowd
    That up her streets in silence hurrying passed,
What manner of death should make their anguish loud,
    What corpse across the funeral pyre be cast,
    For none had spoken it; only, gathering fast
As darkness gathers at noon in the sun's eclipse,
    A shadow of doom enfolded them, vague and vast,
And a cry was heard, unfathered of earthly lips,
"What of the ships, O Carthage? Carthage, what of
    the ships?"

They reached the wall, and nowise strange it seemed
    To find the gates unguarded and open wide;
They climbed the shoulder, and meet enough they deemed
    The black that shrouded the seaward rampart's side
    And veiled in drooping gloom the turrets' pride;
But this was nought, for suddenly down the slope
    They saw the harbour, and sense within them died;
Keel nor mast was there, rudder nor rope;
It lay like a sea-hawk's eyry spoiled of life and hope.

Beyond, where dawn was a glittering carpet, rolled
    From sky to shore on level and endless seas,
Hardly their eyes discerned in a dazzle of gold
    That here in fifties, yonder in twos and threes,
    The ships they sought, like a swarm of drowning bees
By a wanton gust on the pool of a mill-dam hurled,
    Floated forsaken of life-giving tide and breeze,
Their oars broken, their sails for ever furled,
For ever deserted the bulwarks that guarded the wealth of the world.

A moment yet, with breathing quickly drawn
    And hands agrip, the Carthaginian folk
Stared in the bright untroubled face of dawn,
    And strove with vehement heaped denial to choke
    Their sure surmise of fate's impending stroke;
Vainly—for even now beneath their gaze
    A thousand delicate spires of distant smoke
Reddened the disc of the sun with a stealthy haze,
And the smouldering grief of a nation burst with the kindling blaze.

"O dying Carthage!" so their passion raved,
 "Would nought but these the conqueror's hate assuage?
If these be taken, how may the land be saved
 Whose meat and drink was empire, age by age?"
 And bitter memory cursed with idle rage
The greed that coveted gold above renown,
 The feeble hearts that feared their heritage,
The hands that cast the sea-kings' sceptre down
And left to alien brows their famed ancestral crown.

The endless noon, the endless evening through,
 All other needs forgetting, great or small,
They drank despair with thirst whose torment grew
 As the hours died beneath that stifling pall.
 At last they saw the fires to blackness fall
One after one, and slowly turned them home,
 A little longer yet their own to call
A city enslaved, and wear the bonds of Rome,
With weary hearts foreboding all the woe to come.

Minora Sidera

(THE DICTIONARY OF NATIONAL BIOGRAPHY)

SITTING at times over a hearth that burns
  With dull domestic glow,
My thought, leaving the book, gratefully turns
  To you who planned it so.

Not of the great only you deigned to tell—
  The stars by which we steer—
But lights out of the night that flashed, and fell
  To night again, are here

Such as were those, dogs of an elder day,
   Who sacked the golden ports,
And those later who dared grapple their prey
   Beneath the harbour forts:

Some with flag at the fore, sweeping the world
   To find an equal fight,
And some who joined war to their trade, and hurled
   Ships of the line in flight.

Whether their fame centuries long should ring
   They cared not over-much,
But cared greatly to serve God and the king,
   And keep the Nelson touch;

And fought to build Britain above the tide
   Of wars and windy fate;
And passed content, leaving to us the pride
   Of lives obscurely great.

Laudabunt Alii

(AFTER HORACE)

LET others praise, as fancy wills,
   Berlin beneath her trees,
Or Rome upon her seven hills,
   Or Venice by her seas;
Stamboul by double tides embraced,
Or green Damascus in the waste.

For me there's nought I would not leave
    For the good Devon land,
Whose orchards down the echoing cleeve
    Bedewed with spray-drift stand,
And hardly bear the red fruit up
That shall be next year's cider-cup.

You too, my friend, may wisely mark
    How clear skies follow rain,
And, lingering in your own green park
    Or drilled on Laffan's Plain,
Forget not with the festal bowl
To soothe at times your weary soul.

When Drake must bid to Plymouth Hoe
    Good-bye for many a day,
And some were sad that feared to go,
    And some that dared not stay,

Be sure he bade them broach the best,

And raised his tankard with the rest.

" Drake's luck to all that sail with Drake

   For promised lands of gold !

Brave lads, whatever storms may break,

   We've weathered worse of old !

To-night the loving-cup we'll drain,

To-morrow for the Spanish Main ! "

San Stefano

A Ballad of the Bold "Menelaus"

It was morning at St. Helen's, in the great and gallant days,
  And the sea beneath the sun glittered wide,
When the frigate set her courses, all a-shimmer in the haze,
  And she hauled her cable home and took the tide.
She'd a right fighting company, three hundred men and more,
  Nine and forty guns in tackle running free;
And they cheered her from the shore for her colours at the fore,
  When the bold *Menelaus* put to sea.

She'd a right fighting company, three hundred men and more,
  Nine and forty guns in tackle running free ;
And they cheered her from the shore for her colours at the fore,
  When the bold Menelaus *put to sea.*

She was clear of Monte Cristo, she was heading for the land,
  When she spied a pennant red and white and blue ;
They were foemen, and they knew it, and they'd half a league in hand,
  But she flung aloft her royals, and she flew.
She was nearer, nearer, nearer, they were caught beyond a doubt,
  But they slipped her, into Orbetello Bay,
And the lubbers gave a shout as they paid their cables out,
  With the guns grinning round them where they lay.

Now Sir Peter was a captain of a famous fighting race,
  Son and grandson of an admiral was he ;

And he looked upon the batteries, he looked upon the chase,
   And he heard the shout that echoed out to sea.
And he called across the decks, " Ay! the cheering might be late
   If they kept it till the *Menelaus* runs;
Bid the master and his mate heave the lead and lay her straight
   For the prize lying yonder by the guns."

When the summer moon was setting, into Orbetello Bay
   Came the *Menelaus* gliding like a ghost:
And her boats were manned in silence, and in silence pulled away,
   And in silence every gunner took his post.
With a volley from her broadside the citadel she woke,
   And they hammered back like heroes all the night;
But before the morning broke she had vanished through the smoke
   With her prize upon her quarter grappled tight.

It was evening at St. Helen's, in the great and gallant time,
 And the sky behind the down was flushing far;
And the flags were all a-flutter, and the bells were all a-chime,
 When the frigate cast her anchor off the bar.
She'd a right fighting company, three hundred men and more,
 Nine and forty guns in tackle running free;
And they cheered her from the shore for her colours at the fore,
 When the bold *Menelaus* came from sea.

She'd a right fighting company, three hundred men and more,
 Nine and forty guns in tackle running free;
And they cheered her from the shore for her colours at the fore,
 When the bold Menelaus *came from sea.*

Hawke

In seventeen hundred and fifty-nine,
  When Hawke came swooping from the West,
The French King's Admiral with twenty of the line,
  Was sailing forth, to sack us, out of Brest.
The ports of France were crowded, the quays of France a-hum
With thirty thousand soldiers marching to the drum;
For bragging time was over and fighting time was come
  When Hawke came swooping from the West.

'Twas long past noon of a wild November day
  When Hawke came swooping from the West;
He heard the breakers thundering in Quiberon Bay,
  But he flew the flag for battle, line abreast.
Down upon the quicksands roaring out of sight
Fiercely beat the storm-wind, darkly fell the night,
But they took the foe for pilot and the cannon's glare
    for light
  When Hawke came swooping from the West.

The Frenchmen turned like a covey down the wind
  When Hawke came swooping from the West;
One he sank with all hands, one he caught and pinned,
  And the shallows and the storm took the rest.
The guns that should have conquered us they rusted on
    the shore,
The men that would have mastered us they drummed
    and marched no more,
For England was England, and a mighty brood she bore
  When Hawke came swooping from the West.

The Fighting Téméraire

It was eight bells ringing,
 For the morning watch was done,
And the gunner's lads were singing,
 As they polished every gun.
It was eight bells ringing,
And the gunner's lads were singing
For the ship she rode a-swinging,
 As they polished every gun.

Oh! to see the linstock lighting,
 Téméraire! Téméraire!
Oh! to hear the round shot biting,
 Téméraire! Téméraire!
Oh! to see the linstock lighting,
And to hear the round shot biting,
For we're all in love with fighting
 On the Fighting Téméraire.

It was noontide ringing,
 And the battle just begun,
When the ship her way was winging,
 As they loaded every gun.
It was noontide ringing
When the ship her way was winging,
And the gunner's lads were singing
 As they loaded every gun.

There'll be many grim and gory,
 Téméraire! Téméraire!
There'll be few to tell the story,
 Téméraire! Téméraire!
There'll be many grim and gory,
There'll be few to tell the story,
But we'll all be one in glory
 With the Fighting Téméraire.

There's a far bell ringing
 At the setting of the sun,
And a phantom voice is singing
 Of the great days done.
There's a far bell ringing,
And a phantom voice is singing
Of renown for ever clinging
 To the great days done.

Now the sunset breezes shiver,
  Téméraire! Téméraire!
And she's fading down the river,
  Téméraire! Téméraire!
Now the sunset breezes shiver,
And she's fading down the river,
But in England's song for ever
  She's the Fighting Téméraire.

Drake's Drum

Drake he's in his hammock an' a thousand mile away,
    (Capten, art tha sleepin' there below?)
Slung atween the round shot in Nombre Dios Bay,
    An' dreamin' arl the time o' Plymouth Hoe.
Yarnder lumes the Island, yarnder lie the ships,
    Wi' sailor lads a-dancin' heel-an'-toe,
An' the shore-lights flashin', an' the night-tide dashin',
    He sees et arl so plainly as he saw et long ago.

DRAKE'S DRUM

Drake he was a Devon man, an' rüled the Devon seas,
   (Capten, art tha sleepin' there below?),
Rovin' tho' his death fell, he went wi' heart at ease,
   An' dreamin' arl the time o' Plymouth Hoe.
" Take my drum to England, hang et by the shore,
   Strike et when your powder's runnin' low;
If the Dons sight Devon, I'll quit the port o' Heaven,
   An' drum them up the Channel as we drummed them long ago."

Drake he's in his hammock till the great Armadas come,
   (Capten, art tha sleepin' there below?),
Slung atween the round shot, listenin' for the drum,
   An' dreamin' arl the time o' Plymouth Hoe.
Call him on the deep sea, call him up the Sound,
   Call him when ye sail to meet the foe;
Where the old trade's plyin' an' the old flag flyin'
   They shall find him ware an' wakin', as they found him long ago!

Admirals All

Effingham, Grenville, Raleigh, Drake,
   Here's to the bold and free!
Benbow, Collingwood, Byron, Blake,
   Hail to the Kings of the Sea!
Admirals all, for England's sake,
   Honour be yours and fame!
And honour, as long as waves shall break,
   To Nelson's peerless name!

   Admirals all, for England's sake,
      Honour be yours and fame!
   And honour, as long as waves shall break,
      To Nelson's peerless name!

Essex was fretting in Cadiz Bay
   With the galleons fair in sight;
Howard at last must give him his way,
   And the word was passed to fight.
Never was schoolboy gayer than he,
   Since holidays first began:
He tossed his bonnet to wind and sea,
   And under the guns he ran.

Drake nor devil nor Spaniard feared,
   Their cities he put to the sack;
He singed His Catholic Majesty's beard,
   And harried his ships to wrack.
He was playing at Plymouth a rubber of bowls
   When the great Armada came;
But he said, "They must wait their turn, good souls,"
   And he stooped, and finished the game.

Fifteen sail were the Dutchmen bold,
  Duncan he had but two:
But he anchored them fast where the Texel shoaled
  And his colours aloft he flew.
"I've taken the depth to a fathom," he cried.
  And I'll sink with a right good will,
For I know when we're all of us under the tide
  My flag will be fluttering still."

Splinters were flying above, below,
  When Nelson sailed the Sound:
"Mark you, I wouldn't be elsewhere now,"
  Said he, "for a thousand pound!"
The Admiral's signal bade him fly,
  But he wickedly wagged his head,
He clapped the glass to his sightless eye,
  And "I'm damned if I see it," he said.

ADMIRALS ALL

Admirals all, they said their say,
   (The echoes are ringing still)
Admirals all, they went their way
   To the haven under the hill.
But they left us a kingdom none can take,
   The realm of the circling sea,
To be ruled by the rightful sons of Blake
   And the Rodneys yet to be.

Admirals all, for England's sake,
   Honour be yours and fame !
And honour as long as waves shall break
   To Nelson's peerless name !

Gillespie

Riding at dawn, riding alone,
  Gillespie left the town behind;
Before he turned by the Westward road
  A horseman crossed him, staggering blind.

"The Devil's abroad in false Vellore,
  The Devil that stabs by night," he said,
"Women and children, rank and file,
  Dying and dead, dying and dead."

Without a word, without a groan,
   Sudden and swift Gillespie turned,
The blood roared in his ears like fire,
   Like fire the road beneath him burned.

He thundered back to Arcot gate,
   He thundered up through Arcot town,
Before he thought a second thought
   In the barrack yard he lighted down.

"Trumpeter, sound for the Light Dragoons,
   Sound to saddle and spur," he said;
"He that is ready may ride with me,
   And he that can may ride ahead."

Fierce and fain, fierce and fain,
   Behind him went the troopers grim,
They rode as ride the Light Dragoons,
   But never a man could ride with him.

Their rowels ripped their horses' sides,
    Their hearts were red with a deeper goad,
But ever alone before them all
    Gillespie rode, Gillespie rode.

Alone he came to false Vellore,
    The walls were lined, the gates were barred;
Alone he walked where the bullets bit,
    And called above to the Sergeant's Guard.

"Sergeant, Sergeant, over the gate,
    Where are your officers all?" he said;
Heavily came the Sergeant's voice
    "There are two living, and forty dead."

"A rope, a rope," Gillespie cried:
    They bound their belts to serve his need;
There was not a rebel behind the wall
    But laid his barrel and drew his bead.

There was not a rebel among them all
   But pulled his trigger and cursed his aim,
For lightly swung and rightly swung
   Over the gate Gillespie came.

He dressed the line, he led the charge,
   They swept the wall like a stream in spate,
And roaring over the roar they heard
   The galloper guns that burst the gate.

Fierce and fain, fierce and fain,
   The troopers rode the reeking flight:
The very stones remember still
   The end of them that stab by night.

They've kept the tale a hundred years,
   They'll keep the tale a hundred more:
Riding at dawn, riding alone,
   Gillespie came to false Vellore.

Seringapatam

"The sleep that Tippoo Sahib sleeps
    Heeds not the cry of man;
The faith that Tippoo Sahib keeps
    No judge on earth may scan;
He is the lord of whom ye hold
    Spirit and sense and limb,
Fetter and chain are all ye gain
    Who dared to plead with him."

Baird was bonny and Baird was young,
    His heart was strong as steel,
But life and death in the balance hung
    For his wounds were ill to heal.
"Of fifty chains the Sultan gave
    We have filled but forty-nine:
We dare not fail of the perfect tale
    For all Golconda's mine."

That was the hour when Lucas first
    Leapt to his long renown;
Like summer rains his anger burst,
    And swept their scruples down.
"Tell ye the lord to whom ye crouch,
    His fetters bite their fill:
To save your oath I'll wear them both,
    And step the lighter still."

The seasons came, the seasons passed,
    They watched their fellows die ;
But still their thought was forward cast,
    Their courage still was high.
Through tortured days and fevered nights
    Their limbs alone were weak,
And year by year they kept their cheer,
    And spoke as freemen speak.

But once a year, on the fourth of June,
    Their speech to silence died,
And the silence beat to a soundless tune
    And sang with a wordless pride;
Till when the Indian stars were bright,
    And bells at home would ring,
To the fetters' clank they rose and drank
    " England ! God Save the King ! "

SERINGAPATAM

The years came, and the years went,
    The wheel full-circle rolled;
The tyrant's neck must yet be bent,
    The price of blood be told:
The city yet must hear the roar
    Of Baird's avenging guns,
And see him stand with lifted hand
    By Tippoo Sahib's sons.

The lads were bonny, the lads were young,
    But he claimed a pitiless debt;
Life and death in the balance hung,
    They watched it swing and set.
They saw him search with sombre eyes,
    They knew the place he sought;
They saw him feel for the hilted steel,
    They bowed before his thought.

But he—he saw the prison there
    In the old quivering heat,
Where merry hearts had met despair
    And died without defeat;
Where feeble hands had raised the cup
    For feebler lips to drain,
And one had worn with smiling scorn
    His double load of pain.

" The sleep that Tippoo Sahib sleeps
    Hears not the voice of man;
The faith that Tippoo Sahib keeps
    No earthly judge may scan;
For all the wrong your father wrought
    Your father's sons are free;
Where Lucas lay no tongue shall say
    That Mercy bound not me."

A Ballad of John Nicholson

It fell in the year of Mutiny,
 At darkest of the night,
John Nicholson by Jalándhar came,
 On his way to Delhi fight.

And as he by Jalándhar came
 He thought what he must do,
And he sent to the Rajah fair greeting,
 To try if he were true.

"God grant your Highness length of days,
   And friends when need shall be ;
And I pray you send your Captains hither,
   That they may speak with me."

On the morrow through Jalándhar town
   The Captains rode in state ;
They came to the house of John Nicholson
   And stood before the gate.

The chief of them was Mehtab Singh,
   He was both proud and sly ;
His turban gleamed with rubies red,
   He held his chin full high.

He marked his fellows how they put
   Their shoes from off their feet ;
" Now wherefore make ye such ado
   These fallen lords to greet ?

"They have ruled us for a hundred years,
   In truth I know not how,
But though they be fain of mastery,
   They dare not claim it now."

Right haughtily before them all
   The durbar hall he trod,
With rubies red his turban gleamed,
   His feet with pride were shod.

They had not been an hour together,
   A scanty hour or so,
When Mehtab Singh rose in his place
   And turned about to go.

Then swiftly came John Nicholson
   Between the door and him,
With anger smouldering in his eyes
   That made the rubies dim.

"You are overhasty, Mehtab Singh,"—
 Oh, but his voice was low!
He held his wrath with a curb of iron,
 That furrowed cheek and brow.

"You are overhasty, Mehtab Singh,
 When that the rest are gone,
I have a word that may not wait
 To speak with you alone."

The Captains passed in silence forth
 And stood the door behind;
To go before the game was played
 Be sure they had no mind.

But there within John Nicholson
 Turned him on Mehtab Singh,
"So long as the soul is in my body
 You shall not do this thing.

"Have ye served us for a hundred years
   And yet ye know not why?
We brook no doubt of our mastery,
   We rule until we die.

"Were I the one last Englishman
   Drawing the breath of life,
And you the master-rebel of all
   That stir this land to strife—

"Were I," he said, "but a Corporal,
   And you a Rajput King,
So long as the soul was in my body
   You should not do this thing.

"Take off, take off those shoes of pride,
   Carry them whence they came;
Your Captains saw your insolence
   And they shall see your shame."

When Mehtab Singh came to the door
   His shoes they burned his hand,
For there in long and silent lines
   He saw the Captains stand.

When Mehtab Singh rode from the gate
   His chin was on his breast:
The Captains said, " When the strong command
   Obedience is best."

The Guides at Cabul, 1879

Sons of the Island Race, wherever ye dwell,
  Who speak of your fathers' battles with lips that burn,
The deed of an alien legion hear me tell,
  And think not shame from the hearts ye tamed to learn,
  When succour shall fail and the tide for a season turn
To fight with a joyful courage, a passionate pride,
To die at the last as the Guides at Cabul died.

For a handful of seventy men in a barrack of mud,
   Foodless, waterless, dwindling one by one,
Answered a thousand yelling for English blood
   With stormy volleys that swept them gunner from gun,
   And charge on charge in the glare of the Afghan sun,
Till the walls were shattered wherein they crouched at bay,
And dead or dying half of the seventy lay.

Twice they had taken the cannon that wrecked their hold,
   Twice toiled in vain to drag it back,
Thrice they toiled, and alone, wary and bold,
   Whirling a hurricane sword to scatter the rack,
   Hamilton, last of the English, covered their track.
"Never give in!" he cried, and he heard them shout,
And grappled with death as a man that knows not doubt.

And the Guides looked down from their smouldering
   barrack again,
   And behold, a banner of truce, and a voice that spoke:
" Come, for we know that the English all are slain,
   We keep no feud with men of a kindred folk;
   Rejoice with us to be free of the conqueror's yoke."
Silence fell for a moment, then was heard
A sound of laughter and scorn, and an answering word.

" Is it we or the lords we serve who have earned this
      wrong,
   That ye call us to flinch from the battle they bade us
      fight?
We that live—do ye doubt that our hands are strong?
   They that have fallen—ye know that their blood was
      bright!
   Think ye the Guides will barter for lust of the light
The pride of an ancient people in warfare bred,
Honour of comrades living, and faith to the dead?"

Then the joy that spurs the warrior's heart
    To the last thundering gallop and sheer leap
Came on the men of the Guides: they flung apart
    The doors not all their valour could longer keep;
    They dressed their slender line; they breathed deep,
And with never a foot lagging or head bent,
To the clash and clamour and dust of death they went.

The Gay Gordons

(Dargai, October 20th, 1897)

Who's for the Gathering, who's for the Fair?

(Gay goes the Gordon to a fight)

The bravest of the brave are at deadlock there,

(Highlanders ! march ! by the right !)

There are bullets by the hundred buzzing in the air,

There are bonny lads lying on the hillside bare;

But the Gordons know what the Gordons dare

When they hear the pipers playing!

The happiest English heart to-day

   (*Gay goes the Gordon to a fight*)

Is the heart of the Colonel, hide it as he may

   (*Steady there! steady on the right!*)

He sees his work and he sees the way,

He knows his time and the word to say

And he's thinking of the tune that the Gordons play

   When he sets the pipers playing!

Rising, roaring, rushing like the tide,

   (*Gay goes the Gordon to a fight*)

They're up through the fire-zone, not to be denied;

   (*Bayonets! and charge! by the right!*)

Thirty bullets straight where the rest went wide,

And thirty lads are lying on the bare hillside;

But they passed in the hour of the Gordons' pride,

   To the skirl of the pipers' playing.

He Fell Among Thieves

"Ye have robbed," said he, "ye have slaughtered and made an end,
  Take your ill-got plunder, and bury the dead:
What will ye more of your guest and sometime friend?"
  "Blood for our blood," they said.

He laughed: "If one may settle the score for five,
  I am ready; but let the reckoning stand till day:
I have loved the sunlight as dearly as any alive."
  "You shall die at dawn," said they.

HE FELL AMONG THIEVES

He flung his empty revolver down the slope,
    He climbed alone to the Eastward edge of the trees;
All night long in a dream untroubled of hope
    He brooded, clasping his knees.

He did not hear the monotonous roar that fills
    The ravine where the Yassîn river sullenly flows;
He did not see the starlight on the Laspur hills,
    Or the far Afghan snows.

He saw the April noon on his books aglow,
    The wisteria trailing in at the window wide;
He heard his father's voice from the terrace below
    Calling him down to ride.

He saw the gray little church across the park,
    The mounds that hide the loved and honoured dead;
The Norman arch, the chancel softly dark,
    The brasses black and red.

He saw the School Close, sunny and green,
  The runner beside him, the stand by the parapet wall,
The distant tape, and the crowd roaring between
  His own name over all.

He saw the dark wainscot and timbered roof,
  The long tables, and the faces merry and keen;
The College Eight and their trainer dining aloof,
  The Dons on the daïs serene.

He watched the liner's stem ploughing the foam,
  He felt her trembling speed and the thrash of her screw;
He heard her passengers' voices talking of home,
  He saw the flag she flew.

And now it was dawn. He rose strong on his feet,
  And strode to his ruined camp below the wood;
He drank the breath of the morning cool and sweet;
  His murderers round him stood.

Light on the Laspur hills was broadening fast,
  The blood-red snow-peaks chilled to a dazzling white;
He turned, and saw the golden circle at last,
  Cut by the Eastern height.

"O glorious Life, Who dwellest in earth and sun,
  I have lived, I praise and adore Thee."
                    A sword swept.
Over the pass the voices one by one
  Faded, and the hill slept.

Ionicus

With failing feet and shoulders bowed
    Beneath the weight of happier days,
He lagged among the heedless crowd,
    Or crept along suburban ways.
But still through all his heart was young,
    His mood a joy that nought could mar,
A courage, a pride, a rapture, sprung
    Of the strength and splendour of England's war.

From ill-requited toil he turned
> To ride with Picton and with Pack,

Among his grammars inly burned
> To storm the Afghan mountain-track.

When midnight chimed, before Quebec
> He watched with Wolfe till the morning star;

At noon he saw from *Victory's* deck
> The sweep and splendour of England's war.

Beyond the book his teaching sped,
> He left on whom he taught the trace

Of kinship with the deathless dead,
> And faith in all the Island Race.

He passed: his life a tangle seemed,
> His age from fame and power was far;

But his heart was high to the end, and dreamed
> Of the sound and splendour of England's war.

The Non-Combatant

Among a race high-handed, strong of heart,
Sea-rovers, conquerors, builders in the waste,
He had his birth; a nature too complete,
Eager and doubtful, no man's soldier sworn
And no man's chosen captain; born to fail,
A name without an echo: yet he too
Within the cloister of his narrow days
Fulfilled the ancestral rites, and kept alive

The eternal fire; it may be, not in vain:
For out of those who dropped a downward glance
Upon the weakling huddled at his prayers,
Perchance some looked beyond him, and then first
Beheld the glory, and what shrine it filled,
And to what Spirit sacred: or perchance
Some heard him chanting, though but to himself,
The old heroic names: and went their way:
And hummed his music on the march to death.

Clifton Chapel

This is the Chapel: here, my son,
   Your father thought the thoughts of youth,
And heard the words that one by one
   The touch of Life has turned to truth.
Here in a day that is not far
   You too may speak with noble ghosts,
Of manhood and the vows of war
   You made before the Lord of Hosts.

To set the Cause above renown,
>   To love the game beyond the prize,
To honour, while you strike him down,
>   The foe that comes with fearless eyes:
To count the life of battle good,
>   And dear the land that gave you birth,
And dearer yet the brotherhood
>   That binds the brave of all the earth.—

My son, the oath is yours: the end
>   Is His, Who built the world of strife,
Who gave His children Pain for friend,
>   And Death for surest hope of life.
To-day and here the fight's begun,
>   Of the great fellowship you're free;
Henceforth the School and you are one,
>   And what You are, the race shall be.

God send you fortune: yet be sure,
    Among the lights that gleam and pass,
You'll live to follow none more pure
    Than that which glows on yonder brass:
" *Qui procul hinc,*" the legend's writ,—
    The frontier-grave is far away—
" *Qui ante diem periit :*
    Sed miles, sed pro patriâ."

England

Praise thou with praise unending
    The Master of the Wine;
To all their portions sending
    Himself he mingled thine:

The sea-born flush of morning,
    The sea-born hush of night,
The East wind comfort scorning,
    And the North wind driving right:

The world for gain and giving,
    The game for man and boy,
The life that joys in living,
    The faith that lives in joy.

The Echo

OF A BALLAD SUNG BY H. PLUNKET GREENE TO
HIS OLD SCHOOL

TWICE three hundred boys were we,
  Long ago, long ago,
Where the Downs look out to the Severn Sea.
  Clifton for aye !
We held by the game and hailed the team,
For many could play where few could dream.
  Bonny St. Johnston stands on Tay.

Some were for profit and some for pride,
  Long ago, long ago,
Some for the flag they lived and died.
  Clifton for aye !

The work of the world must still be done,

And minds are many though truth be one.

Bonny St. Johnston stands on Tay.

But a lad there was to his fellows sang,

Long ago, long ago,

And soon the world to his music rang.

Clifton for aye!

Follow your Captains, crown your Kings,

But what will ye give to the lad that sings?

Bonny St. Johnston stands on Tay.

For the voice ye hear is the voice of home,

Long ago, long ago,

And the voice of Youth with the world to roam.

Clifton for aye!

The voice of passion and human tears,

And the voice of the vision that lights the years.

Bonny St. Johnston stands on Tay.

Vitaï Lampada

There's a breathless hush in the Close to-night—
　Ten to make and the match to win—
A bumping pitch and a blinding light,
　An hour to play and the last man in.
And it's not for the sake of a ribboned coat,
　Or the selfish hope of a season's fame,
But his Captain's hand on his shoulder smote
　"Play up! play up! and play the game!"

The sand of the desert is sodden red,—
    Red with the wreck of a square that broke;—
The Gatling's jammed and the Colonel dead,
    And the regiment blind with dust and smoke.
The river of death has brimmed his banks,
    And England's far, and Honour a name,
But the voice of a schoolboy rallies the ranks:
    " Play up! play up! and play the game!"

This is the word that year by year,
    While in her place the School is set,
Every one of her sons must hear,
    And none that hears it dare forget.
This they all with a joyful mind
    Bear through life like a torch in flame,
And falling fling to the host behind—
    " Play up! play up! and play the game!'

A Song of Exmoor

THE Forest above and the Combe below,
   On a bright September morn!
He's the soul of a clod who thanks not God
   That ever his body was born!
So hurry along, the stag's afoot,
   The Master's up and away!
Halloo! Halloo! we'll follow it through
   From Bratton to Porlock Bay!

   So hurry along, the stag's afoot,
      The Master's up and away!
   Halloo! Halloo! we'll follow it through
      From Bratton to Porlock Bay!

Hark to the tufters' challenge true,
  'Tis a note that the red-deer knows!
His courage awakes, his covert he breaks,
  And up for the moor he goes!
He's all his rights and seven on top,
  His eye's the eye of a king,
And he'll beggar the pride of some that ride
  Before he leaves the ling!

Here comes Antony bringing the pack,
  Steady! he's laying them on!
By the sound of their chime you may tell that it's time
  To harden your heart and be gone.
Nightacott, Narracott, Hunnacott's passed,
  Right for the North they race:
He's leading them straight for Blackmoor Gate,
  And he's setting a pounding pace!

We're running him now on a breast-high scent,
   But he leaves us standing still;
When we swing round by Westland Pound
   He's far up Challacombe Hill.
The pack are a string of struggling ants,
   The quarry's a dancing midge,
They're trying their reins on the edge of the Chains
   While he's on Cheriton Ridge.

He's gone by Kittuck and Lucott Moor,
   He's gone by Woodcock's Ley;
By the little white town he's turned him down,
   And he's soiling in open sea.
So hurry along, we'll both be in,
   The crowd are a parish away!
We're a field of two, and we've followed it through
   From Bratton to Porlock Bay!

So hurry along, we'll both be in,
The crowd are a parish away;
We've a field of two, aud we've followed it through
From Bratton to Porlock Bay!

Fidele's Grassy Tomb

The Squire sat propped in a pillowed chair,
His eyes were alive and clear of care,
But well he knew that the hour was come
To bid good-bye to his ancient home.

He looked on garden, wood, and hill,
He looked on the lake, sunny and still;
The last of earth that his eyes could see
Was the island church of Orchardleigh.

The last that his heart could understand
Was the touch of the tongue that licked his hand:
" Bury the dog at my feet," he said,
And his voice dropped, and the Squire was dead.

Now the dog was a hound of the Danish breed,
Staunch to love and strong at need:
He had dragged his master safe to shore
When the tide was ebbing at Elsinore.

From that day forth, as reason would,
He was named " Fidele," and made it good:
When the last of the mourners left the door
Fidele was dead on the chantry floor.

They buried him there at his master's feet,
And all that heard of it deemed it meet:
The story went the round for years,
Till it came at last to the Bishop's ears.

FIDELE'S GRASSY TOMB

Bishop of Bath and Wells was he,
Lord of the lords of Orchardleigh;
And he wrote to the Parson the strongest screed
That Bishop may write or Parson read.

The sum of it was that a soulless hound
Was known to be buried in hallowed ground:
From scandal sore the Church to save
They must take the dog from his master's grave.

The heir was far in a foreign land,
The Parson was wax to my Lord's command:
He sent for the Sexton and bade him make
A lonely grave by the shore of the lake.

The Sexton sat by the water's brink
Where he used to sit when he used to think:
He reasoned slow, but he reasoned it out,
And his argument left him free from doubt.

"A Bishop," he said, "is the top of his trade:
But there's others can give him a start with the spade:.
Yon dog, he carried the Squire ashore,
And a Christian couldn't ha' done no more."

The grave was dug; the mason came
And carved on stone Fidele's name:
But the dog that the Sexton laid inside
Was a dog that never had lived or died.

So the Parson was praised, and the scandal stayed,
Till, a long time after, the church decayed,
And, laying the floor anew, they found
In the tomb of the Squire the bones of a hound.

As for the Bishop of Bath and Wells
No more of him the story tells;
Doubtless he lived as a Prelate and Prince,
And died and was buried a century since.

And whether his view was right or wrong

Has little to do with this my song;

Something we owe him, you must allow;

And perhaps he has changed his mind by now.

The Squire in the family chantry sleeps,

The marble still his memory keeps:

Remember, when the name you spell,

There rest Fidele's bones as well.

For the Sexton's grave you need not search,

'Tis a nameless mound by the island church:

An ignorant fellow, of humble lot—

But he knew one thing that a Bishop did not.

Gavotte

(OLD FRENCH)

MEMORIES long in music sleeping,
   No more sleeping,
     No more dumb;
Delicate phantoms softly creeping
   Softly back from the old-world come.

Faintest odours around them straying,
   Suddenly straying
     In chambers dim;
Whispering silks in order swaying,
   Glimmering gems on shoulders slim:

GAVOTTE

Courage advancing strong and tender,
   Grace untender
      Fanning desire;
Suppliant conquest, proud surrender,
   Courtesy cold of hearts on fire—

Willowy billowy now they're bending,
   Low they're bending
      Down-dropt eyes;
Stately measure and stately ending,
   Music sobbing, and a dream that dies.

Imogen

(A Lady of Tender Age)

LADIES, where were your bright eyes glancing,
   Where were they glancing yesternight?
Saw ye Imogen dancing, dancing,
   Imogen dancing all in white?
   Laughed she not with a pure delight,
   Laughed she not with a joy serene,
Stepped she not with a grace entrancing,
   Slenderly girt in silken sheen?

All through the night from dusk to daytime
    Under her feet the hours were swift,
Under her feet the hours of playtime
    Rose and fell with a rhythmic lift :
    Music set her adrift, adrift,
    Music eddying towards the day
Swept her along as brooks in Maytime
    Carry the freshly falling May.

Ladies, life is a changing measure,
    Youth is a lilt that endeth soon ;
Pluck ye never so fast at pleasure,
    Twilight follows the longest noon.
    Nay, but here is a lasting boon,
    Life for hearts that are old and chill,
Youth undying for hearts that treasure
    Imogen dancing, dancing still.

Nel Mezzo del Cammìn

WHISPER it not that late in years

Sorrow shall fade and the world be brighter,

Life be freed of tremor and tears,

Heads be wiser and hearts be lighter.

Ah! but the dream that all endears,

The dream we sell for your pottage of truth—

Give us again the passion of youth,

Sorrow shall fade and the world be brighter.

The Invasion

Spring, they say, with his greenery
Northward marches at last,
Mustering thorn and elm;
Breezes rumour him conquering,
Tell how Victory sits
High on his glancing helm.

THE INVASION

Smit with sting of his archery,

    Hardest ashes and oaks

        Burn at the root below:

Primrose, violet, daffodil,

    Start like blood where the shafts

        Light from his golden bow.

Here where winter oppresses us

    Still we listen and doubt,

        Dreading a hope betrayed:

Sore we long to be greeting him,

    Still we linger and doubt

        " What if his march be stayed?"

Folk in thrall to the enemy,

    Vanquished, tilling a soil

        Hateful and hostile grown:

Always wearily, warily,
  Feeding deep in the heart
    Passion they dare not own—

So we wait the deliverer;
  Surely soon shall he come,
    Soon shall his hour be due:
Spring shall come with his greenery,
  Life be lovely again,
    Earth be the home we knew.

Pereunt et Imputantur

(After Martial)

Bernard, if to you and me
   Fortune all at once should give
Years to spend secure and free,
   With the choice of how to live,
Tell me, what should we proclaim
Life deserving of the name?

Winning some one else's case?
   Saving some one else's seat?
Hearing with a solemn face
   People of importance bleat?
No, I think we should not still
Waste our time at others' will.

Summer noons beneath the limes,
   Summer rides at evening cool,
Winter's tales and home-made rhymes,
   Figures on the frozen pool—
These would we for labours take,
And of these our business make.

Ah! but neither you nor I
   Dare in earnest venture so:
Still we let the good days die
   And to swell the reckoning go.
What are those that know the way,
Yet to walk therein delay?

Felix Antonius

(AFTER MARTIAL)

To-day, my friend is seventy-five;
   He tells his tale with no regret;
   His brave old eyes are steadfast yet,
His heart the lightest heart alive.

He sees behind him green and wide
   The pathway of his pilgrim years;
   He sees the shore, and dreadless hears
The whisper of the creeping tide.

For out of all his days, not one
    Has passed and left its unlaid ghost
    To seek a light for ever lost,
Or wail a deed for ever done.

So for reward of life-long truth
    He lives again, as good men can,
    Redoubling his allotted span
With memories of a stainless youth.

The Last Word

Before the April night was late
A rider came to the castle gate;
A rider breathing human breath,
But the words he spoke were the words of Death.

"Greet you well from the King our lord,
He marches hot for the eastward ford;
Living or dying, all or one,
Ye must keep the ford till the race be run."

THE LAST WORD

Sir Alain rose with lips that smiled,
He kissed his wife, he kissed his child:
Before the April night was late
Sir Alain rode from the castle gate.

He called his men-at-arms by name,
But one there was uncalled that came:
He bade his troop behind him ride,
But there was one that rode beside.

" Why will you spur so fast to die ?
Be wiser ere the night go by.
A message late is a message lost;
For all your haste the foe had crossed.

" Are men such small unmeaning things
To strew the board of smiling Kings ?
With life and death they play their game,
And life or death, the end's the same."

Softly the April air above
Rustled the woodland homes of love:
Softly the April air below
Carried the dream of buds that blow.

" Is he that bears a warrior's fame
To shun the pointless stroke of shame ?
Will he that propped a trembling throne
Not stand for right when right's his own ?

" Your oath on the four gospels sworn ?
What oath can bind resolves unborn ?
You lose that far eternal life ?
Is it yours to lose ? Is it child and wife ?"

But now beyond the pathway's bend,
Sir Alain saw the forest end,
And winding wide beneath the hill,
The glassy river lone and still.

And now he saw with lifted eyes
The East like a great chancel rise,
And deep through all his senses drawn,
Received the sacred wine of dawn.

He set his face to the stream below,
He drew his axe from the saddle bow:
" Farewell, Messire, the night is sped;
There lies the ford, when all is said."

Ireland, Ireland

Down thy valleys, Ireland, Ireland,
   Down thy valleys green and sad,
Still thy spirit wanders wailing,
   Wanders wailing, wanders mad.

Long ago that anguish took thee,
   Ireland, Ireland, green and fair,
Spoilers strong in darkness took thee,
   Broke thy heart and left thee there.

Down thy valleys, Ireland, Ireland,
   Still thy spirit wanders mad;
All too late they love that wronged thee,
   Ireland, Ireland, green and sad.

Moonset

Past seven o'clock: time to be gone;
Twelfth-night's over and dawn shivering up:
A hasty cut of the loaf, a steaming cup,
Down to the door, and there is Coachman John.

Ruddy of cheek is John, and bright of eye;
But John it appears has none of your grins and winks;
Civil enough, but short: perhaps he thinks:
Words come once in a mile, and always dry.

Has he a mind or not? I wonder; but soon
We turn through a leafless wood, and there to the right,
Like a sun bewitched in alien realms of night,
Mellow and yellow and rounded hangs the moon.

Strangely near she seems, and terribly great:

The world is dead: why are we travelling still?

Nightmare silence grips my struggling will;

We are driving for ever and ever to find a gate.

"When you come to consider the moon," says John at last,

And stops, to feel his footing and take his stand;

"And then there's some will say there's never a hand

That made the world!"

                A flick, and the gates are passed.

Out of the dim magical moonlit park,

Out to the workday road and wider skies:

There's a warm flush in the East where day's to rise,

And I'm feeling the better for Coachman John's remark.

Hymn

In the Time of War and Tumults

O Lord Almighty, Thou whose hands
   Despair and victory give;
In whom, though tyrants tread their lands,
   The souls of nations live;

Thou wilt not turn Thy face away
   From those who work Thy will,
But send Thy peace on hearts that pray,
   And guard Thy people still.

Remember not the days of shame,
   The hands with rapine dyed,
The wavering will, the baser aim,
   The brute material pride:

Remember, Lord, the years of faith,
  The spirits humbly brave,
The strength that died defying death,
  The love that loved the slave:

The race that strove to rule Thine earth
  With equal laws unbought:
Who bore for Truth the pangs of birth,
  And brake the bonds of Thought.

Remember how, since time began,
  Thy dark eternal mind
Through lives of men that fear not man
  Is light for all mankind.

Thou wilt not turn Thy face away
  From those who work Thy will,
But send Thy strength on hearts that pray
  For strength to serve Thee still.

The Building of the Temple

(AN ANTHEM HEARD IN CANTERBURY CATHEDRAL)

The Organ.

O LORD our God, we are strangers before Thee, and sojourners, as were all our fathers: our days on the earth are as a shadow, and there is none abiding.

O Lord God of our fathers, keep this for ever in the imagination of the thoughts of Thy people, and prepare their heart unto Thee.

And give unto Solomon my son a perfect heart to keep Thy commandments, and to build the palace for the which I have made provision.

Boys' voices.

O come to the Palace of Life,

Let us build it again.

It was founded on terror and strife,

It was laid in the curse of the womb,

And pillared on toil and pain,

And hung with veils of doom,

And vaulted with the darkness of the tomb.

Men's voices.

O Lord our God, we are sojourners here for a day,

Strangers and sojourners, as all our fathers were:

Our years on the earth are a shadow that fadeth away;

Grant us light for our labour, and a time for prayer.

Boys.

But now with endless song,

And joy fulfilling the Law;

Of passion as pure as strong

And pleasure undimmed of awe;

With garners of wine and grain

Laid up for the ages long,

Let us build the Palace again
And enter with endless song,
Enter and dwell secure, forgetting the years of wrong.

Men.

O Lord our God, we are strangers and sojourners here,
  Our beginning was night, and our end is hid in Thee:
Our labour on the earth is hope redeeming fear,
  In sorrow we build for the days we shall not see.

Boys.

      Great is the name
      Of the strong and skilled,
      Lasting the fame
      Of them that build:
      The tongues of many nations
      Shall speak of our praise,
      And far generations
      Be glad for our days.

Men.
We are sojourners here as all our fathers were,
  As all our children shall be, forgetting and forgot :
The fame of man is a murmur that passeth on the air,
  We perish indeed if Thou remember not.

We are sojourners here as all our fathers were,
  Strangers travelling down to the land of death :
There is neither work nor device nor knowledge there,
  O grant us might for our labour, and to rest in faith.

Boys.
In joy, in the joy of the light to be,

Men.
O Father of Lights, unvarying and true,

Boys.
Let us build the Palace of Life anew.

Men.
Let us build for the years we shall not see.

Boys.

Lofty of line and glorious of hue,

With gold and pearl and with the cedar tree,

Men.

With silence due

And with service free,

Boys.

Let us build it for ever in splendour new.

Men.

Let us build in hope and in sorrow, and rest in Thee.

Notes

The Quarter-Gunner's Yarn. This ballad is founded on fragmentary lines communicated to the author by Admiral Sir Windham Hornby, K.C.B., who served under Sir Thomas Hardy in 1827.

Væ Victis. See *Livy*, xxx., 43, *Diodorus Siculus*, xix., 106.

San Stefano. Sir Peter Parker was the son of Admiral Christopher Parker, grandson of Admiral Sir Peter Parker (the life-long friend and chief mourner of Nelson), and great-grandson of Admiral Sir William Parker. On his mother's side he was grandson of Admiral Byron, and first cousin of Lord Byron, the poet. He was killed in action near Baltimore in 1814, and buried in St. Margaret's, Westminster, where may be seen the monument erected to his memory by the officers of the *Menelaus*.

The Fighting Téméraire. The two last stanzas have been misunderstood. It seems, therefore, necessary to state that they are intended to refer to Turner's picture in the National Gallery of " The Fighting *Téméraire* Tugged to her Last Berth."

Drake's Drum. A state drum, painted with the arms of Sir Francis Drake, is preserved among other relics at Buckland Abbey, the seat of the Drake family in Devon.

NOTES 119

Seringapatam. In 1780, while attempting to relieve Arcot, a British force of three thousand men was cut to pieces by Hyder Ali. Baird, then a young captain in the 73rd, was left for dead on the field. He was afterwards, with forty-nine other officers, kept in prison at Seringapatam, and treated with Oriental barbarity and treachery by Hyder Ali and his son Tippoo Sahib, Sultans of Mysore. Twenty-three of the prisoners died by poison, torture, and fever; the rest were surrendered in 1784. In 1799, at the siege of Seringapatam, Major-General Baird commanded the first European brigade, and volunteered to lead the storming column. Tippoo Sahib, with eight thousand of his men, fell in the assault, but the victor spared the lives of his sons and forbade a general sack of the city.

Clifton Chapel. Clifton is one of the two schools from which the largest number of boys pass direct into the R. M. A., Woolwich, and R. M. C., Sandhurst. Thirty-five Old Cliftonian officers served in the late campaign on the Indian Frontier, of whom twenty-two were mentioned in despatches and six recommended for the Distinguished Service Order. The connection of the school with Egypt and the Soudan is hardly less memorable.

The Echo. The ballad was "The Twa Sisters of Binnorie," as set by Arthur Somervell.

ADMIRALS ALL. Fourteenth Edition.

SOME PRESS NOTICES.

"Several of these songs, we venture to say, will take an eminent and enduring place among our patriotic poetry. The literature of the Navy in particular is enriched with some numbers more spirit-stirring than anything that has appeared since Tennyson's immortal Ballad of the 'Revenge.' Mr. Newbolt's style, indeed, has not the volume and impetus of Mr. Kipling's, but it is simpler and more concise, and has more of true lyric, as distinct from rhetorical quality. More than one of his songs ought to be set to music, and that by our best composers. . . . If ever poem carried its own melody, it is 'Drake's Drum.' . . . If we should fall beneath our former selves when the great Armadas come, it will not be for want of a singer to pipe us to quarters. . . . Every bit as good as the sea songs is the 'Ballad of John Nicholson' [quoted]. If this be not ballad poetry of the right strain, we know not where to look for it. Mr. Newbolt ennobles the good old sea song of our ancestors by adding to its swing and spirit a fervour of imagination and a literary finish in which it has hitherto been lacking."—*Daily Chronicle.*

"Mr. Newbolt essays the ballad simple and direct, and it is no little praise to him that in assuming topics and methods which have recently become identified so closely with Mr. Kipling, he nevertheless succeeds in striking an entirely original note. . . . When he is well set in a swinging metre, Mr. Newbolt's verve and virility are tremendous. . . . Here are all the qualities of ballad poetry—simplicity, directness, a vivid impression, and the quick sympathy which leaps from word to eye, and makes every reader yearn to be up and doing.—*Literature.*"

"Genuinely inspired pieces. . . . . What strikes a critic most of all, in Mr. Newbolt's work, is its mixture of restraint and strength with flexibility of verse and real power of expression; while it is pervaded by the aim of glorifying great things and great men, and has no tinge of the pessimism, cynicism, or morbidity of the day."—*St. James's Gazette.*

"Mr. Cory wrote patriotic verse ten years ago, in the very spirit which Mr. Newbolt has so admirably caught. But where ten years ago was the public to send such a book triumphantly into its fourteenth edition? It did not exist. And therefore, after reading 'Admirals All,' and noting the success it has won, a fair critic owes his thanks to the Navy League for creating (or at least enlarging) the demand, as well as to Mr. Newbolt for supplying it. Mr. Newbolt is of the true line of Cory, Doyle, and Lyall."—A. T. Q. C., in *Speaker.*

List of Books
PUBLISHED BY
ELKIN MATHEWS

TELEGRAPHIC
ADDRESS—

"ELEGANTIA,
LONDON."

MOST OF THE BOOKS IN THIS CATALOGUE ARE
PUBLISHED AT NET PRICES

LONDON: VIGO STREET, W.

1898-9

Vigo Viatica
Lector! eme, lege, & gaudebis

List of Books
IN
BELLES LETTRES
(Including some Importations and Transfers)

PUBLISHED BY

Elkin Mathews
VIGO STREET, LONDON, W.

N.B.—The Authors and Publisher reserve the right of reprinting any book in this list, except in cases where a stipulation has been made to the contrary, and of printing a separate edition of any of the books for America. In the case of limited Editions, the numbers mentioned do not include the copies sent for review, nor those supplied to the public libraries. The prices of books not yet published are subject to variation.

The Books mentioned in this Catalogue can be obtained to order by any Bookseller. It should be noted also that most of them are supplied to the Trade on terms which will not allow of discount.

※§§◦

The following are a few of the Authors represented in this Catalogue

LAURENCE BINYON.	LIONEL JOHNSON.
R. D. BLACKMORE.	P. B. MARSTON.
ROBERT BRIDGES.	WILLIAM MORRIS.
BLISS CARMAN.	HENRY NEWBOLT.
E. R. CHAPMAN.	HON. RODEN NOEL.
WALTER CRANE.	STEPHEN PHILLIPS.
GEO. DARLEY.	MAY PROBYN.
CANON DIXON.	F. YORK POWELL.
MICHAEL FIELD.	WILLIAM STRANG.
T. GORDON HAKE.	J. A. SYMONDS.
ARTHUR HALLAM.	HENRY VAN DYKE.
W. C. HAZLITT.	E. H. LACON WATSON.
KATHARINE HINKSON.	THEODORE WATTS DUNTON.
HERBERT P. HORNE.	FREDERICK WEDMORE.
RICHARD HOVEY.	P. H. WICKSTEED.
SELWYN IMAGE.	W. B. YEATS.

ABBOTT (DR.). THE BIRDS ABOUT US 73 Engravings. Second Edition. Thick cr. 8vo. 5s. 6d. net.

TRAVELS IN A TREE-TOP. Sm. 8vo. 5s. net.

"Dr. Abbott pleases by the interest he takes in the subject which he treats . . . and he adorns his matter with a good English style. . . . Altogether, with its dainty printing, it would be a charming book to read in the open air on a bright summer's day."—*Athenæum*.

"He has an observant eye, a warm sympathy, and a pen that enables us to see with him. Nothing could be more restful than to read the thoughts of such naturelovers. The very titles of his chapters suggest quiet and gentle things."—*Dublin Herald*.

"A delightful volume this of Nature Sketches. Dr. Abbott writes about New England woods and streams, scenes neither familiar nor quite strange to us who know the same things in the old country. The severer winter makes some difference, as, for instance, in the number of birds that migrate there, but are stationary here; and there are, of course, other differences in both fauna and flora; nevertheless, we feel, in a way, at home, when Dr. Abbott takes us on one of his delightful winter or summer excursions. This is a book which we cannot recommend too highly."—*Spectator*.

ARMOUR (MARGARET). THAMES SONNETS AND SEMBLANCES. By Mrs. W. B. MACDOUGALL (MARGARET ARMOUR). With 12 full-page Illustrations, Decorated Title-page and Tail-piece by W. B. MACDOUGALL. Fcap. 4to. 5s. net.

ARNOLD (MATTHEW). See GALTON.

BABY LAYS. By ADA STOW. With 16 Pictures, by EDITH CALVERT. Royal 16mo. 1s. 6d. net.
[*Third Thousand.*

"A book of fresh nursery rhymes, all very good and very nonsensical, as they ought to be. The Bedford Park school of illustration suits them admirably, and the one fits the other like a hand to a glove."—*Booksellers' Review*.

"You can think around one of these fables for an eight hours day."—DAGONET, in the *Referee*.

"Contains verses far superior both in invention and technique to the general run . . . . There is humour in these and delicate fancy."—*Daily News*.

Baby Lays, More. BY ADA STOW, 14 Pictures by EDITH CALVERT. Royal 16mo. 1s. 6d. net.

BALLADS AND ETCHINGS. A BOOK OF BALLADS. By ALICE SARGANT. With 5 Etchings by WILLIAM STRANG. Medium 4to. 15s. net.

BATEMAN (MAY). SONNETS AND SONGS. With a title design by JOHN D. MACKENZIE. Fcap. 8vo. 3s. 6d. net.

BEARDSLEY (AUBREY). *See* BJORNSON *and* RUDING.

BINYON (LAURENCE). LYRIC POEMS, with title-page by SELWYN IMAGE. Sq. 16mo. 5s. net.

See THE GARLAND.

BJORNSON (B.). PASTOR SANG : being the Norwegian Drama, Over Ævne. Frontispiece by AUBREY BEARDSLEY. Fcap. 8vo. 3s. 6d. net.

BLACKMORE (R. D.). FRINGILLA ; OR, SOME TALES IN VERSE. By the Author of "Lorna Doone." With Eleven full-page Illustrations and numerous vignettes and initials by L. FAIRFAX-MUCKLEY. Sm. 4to. 10s. net.

BOND (R. WARWICK). ANOTHER SHEAF. With Photogravure Frontispiece. Cr. 8vo. 2s. 6d. net.

BOURCHIER (M.). THE ADVENTURES OF A GOLDSMITH. A Historical Romance. By the Author of "The C Major of Life." Cr. 8vo. 6s. [*Second Edition.*

"Really admirable. Mr. Bourchier possesses pre-eminently the gift of expression ; he uses words with extraordinary discrimination, and clothes an idea or creates a picture with exceptional originality, vividness, and force. His character drawing also is by no means without insight. The scene is laid in Paris, in the time of the First Consul, and the atmosphere is thickly charged with political intrigue. A detailed knowledge of the internal history of France is necessary to the reader who would understand the politics of the book. And the reader who would be content to take these for granted will find some little trouble in following the thread of the story. The lover of the historical novel will be well advised to take this trouble. He will be repaid not only by the excellencies already mentioned, but by sundry strikingly dramatic situations which are developed to the utmost."—*World.*

"A new novel from the author of 'The C Major of Life' will be welcomed by all who had the good fortune to read that clever and thoughtful work, and can hardly fail to rivet the attention of those who now make trial for the first time of Mr. Bourchier's skill in handling narrative, dialogue, and plot. . . . It is a work of outstanding merit, not merely in virtue of the fine literary quality of the writing, but of the subtlety of observation and keen dramatic instinct with which the author has turned to account his historical studies of the period."—*Spectator.*

THE C MAJOR OF LIFE : A Novel. Cr. 8vo. 3s. 6d.

BRETON (NICHOLAS). *See* ISHAM FACSIMILE REPRINTS.

BRIDGES (J. A.). IN A VILLAGE (POEMS). Printed at the CHISWICK PRESS. Crown 8vo. 5s. net.

BRIDGES (ROBERT). See THE GARLAND.

BROWNE (H. DEVEY). PAPERS FROM PUNCH, IN PROSE AND VERSE. With Illustrations by G. DU MAURIER, LINLEY SAMBOURNE, J. BERNARD PARTRIDGE, and others. Crown 8vo. 3s. 6d.

CALVERT (EDITH). See BABY LAYS and MORE BABY LAYS.

CANON (THE): An Exposition of the Pagan Mystery perpetuated in the Cabala as the Rule of all the Arts. With a Preface by R. B. CUNNINGHAME GRAHAM. Demy 8vo. Over 400 pp., with numerous Illustrations. 12s. net.

CARMAN (BLISS). LOW TIDE ON GRAND PRÉ: a Book of Lyrics. Second Edition. Small 8vo. 3s. 6d. net.

BEHIND THE ARRAS: A BOOK OF THE UNSEEN. With designs by T. B. METEYARD. Fcap. 8vo. 5s. net.

"A strange, restless, decidedly impressive book, with a lurid glow about the lyrics it contains. Mr. Carman's vocabulary is rich and exotic. . . . The book contains rich poetical ore. . . . .It is sumptuously printed, and strikingly bound."
—*Pall Mall Gazette.*

"A brilliant and free fancy decorates the fabric of his thoughts, as though the wind should wave the arras and yield us glimpses of undying roses."—*Speaker.*

CARMAN (BLISS) and RICHARD HOVEY. MORE SONGS FROM VAGABONDIA. With Decorations by TOM B. METEYARD. Fcap. 8vo. 5s. net.

SONGS FROM VAGABONDIA. [*Sold out.*

"These little snatches have the spirit of a gipsy Omar Khayyám. They have always careless verve, and often careless felicity; they are masculine and rough, as roving songs should be. . . . Here, certainly, is the poet's soul. . . . You have the whole spirit of the book in such an unforgetable little lyric as 'In the House of Idiedaily.' . . . We refer the reader to the delightful little volume itself, which comes as a welcome interlude amidst the highly wrought introspective poetry of the day."—FRANCIS THOMPSON, in *Merry England.*

CHAPMAN (ELIZABETH RACHEL). A LITTLE CHILD'S WREATH : A Sonnet Sequence. With title-page and cover designed by SELWYN IMAGE. Second Edition. Sq. 16mo., green buckram. 3s. 6d. net.

"Contains many tender and pathetic passages, and some really exquisite and subtle touches of childhood nature. . . . The average excellence of the sonnets is undoubted."—*Spectator.*

COLERIDGE (HON. STEPHEN). THE SANCTITY OF CONFESSION: A Romance. 2nd edition. Cr. 8vo. 2s. 6d [*Very few remain.*]

Mr. GLADSTONE writes:—"I have read the singularly well told story. . . . It opens up questions both deep and dark; it cannot be right to accept in religion or anything else a secret which destroys the life of an innocent fellow creature."

CORBIN (JOHN). THE ELIZABETHAN HAMLET: A Study of the Sources, and of Shakspere's Environment, to show that the Mad Scenes had a Comic Aspect now Ignored. With a Prefatory Note by F. YORK POWELL, Regius Professor of Modern History at the University of Oxford. Small 4to. 3s. 6d. net.

CRANE (WALTER). SLATE AND PENCIL-VANIA Adventures in a Desert Island. Decyphered in 26 coloured Pictures by WALTER CRANE. 4to., 1885, 3s. 6d. net.

POTHOOKS AND PERSEVERANCE; or, The A B C Serpent. Penned and adorned with 24 coloured Pictures by WALTER CRANE. 4to., 1886. 3s. 6d. net.

Transferred to the present Publisher.

UNDER THE HAWTHORN, AND OTHER VERSES. By A. DE GRUCHY. With Frontispiece by WALTER CRANE. Cr. 8vo. 5s. net.

IN THE FIRE, AND OTHER FANCIES. By EFFIE JOHNSON. With frontispiece by WALTER CRANE. Imperial 16mo. 3s. 6d. net.

A SICILIAN IDYLL. By JOHN TODHUNTER. With Frontispiece by WALTER CRANE. Imp. 16mo. 5s. net. A few L. P. copies. 10s. 6d. net.

DANTE. LA COMMEDIA DI DANTE. A New Text carefully Revised with the aid of the most recent Editions and Collations. Printed by CONSTABLES. Thick Fcap. 8vo. 4s. 6d. net.

DANTE. SIX SERMONS. By P. H. WICKSTEED. Cr. 8vo. 2s. net. [Fourth Edition.

DANTE and His Early Biographers. By EDWARD MOORE, D.D. Crown 8vo. 3s. 6d. net.
Transferred to the present Publisher.

DANTE. See SCHAFF.

DARLEY (GEORGE). NEPENTHE: a Poem in Two Cantos. With an Introduction by R. A. STREATFEILD. Fcap. 8vo. 2s. 6d. net.

DIXON (REV. CANON). See THE GARLAND.

DOWSON (ERNEST). DILEMMAS: Stories and Studies in Sentiment. (A Case of Conscience.—The Diary of a Successful Man.—An Orchestral Violin.—The Statute of Limitations.—Souvenirs of an Egoist). Crown 8vo. 3s. 6d.

DUBLIN VERSES. By MEMBERS OF TRINITY COLLEGE. Selected and Edited by H. A. HINKSON, late Scholar of Trinity College, Dublin. Pott 4to. 5s. net.

Includes contributions by the following:—Aubrey de Vere, Sir Stephen de Vere, Oscar Wilde, J. K. Ingram, A. P. Graves, J. Todhunter, W. E. H. Lecky, T. W. Rolleston, Edward Dowden, G. A. Greene, Savage-Armstrong, Douglas Hyde, R. Y. Tyrrell, G. N. Plunkett, W. Macneile Dixon, William Wilkins, George Wilkins, and Edwin Hamilton.

"A pleasant volume of contemporary Irish Verse... A judicious selection."
—*Times*.

"Wherever there is a group of Irish readers in near or far-off lands, these 'Dublin Verses' will be sure to command attention and applause."—*Glasgow Herald*.

FIELD (MICHAEL). SIGHT AND SONG (Poems on Pictures). Printed by CONSTABLES. 12mo. 5s. *net.*
[*Very few remain.*]

STEPHANIA: A TRIALOGUE IN THREE ACTS. Frontispiece, colophon, and ornament for binding designed by SELWYN IMAGE. Printed by FOLKARD & SON. Pott 4to. 6s. *net.* [*Very few remain.*]

"We have true drama in 'Stephania.' . . . . Stephania, Otho, and Sylvester II., the three persons of the play, are more than mere names. . . . . Besides great effort, commendable effort, there is real greatness in this play; and the blank verse is often sinewy and strong with thought and passion."—*Speaker.*

"'Stephania' is striking in design and powerful in execution. It is a highly dramatic 'trialogue' between the Emperor Otho III., his tutor Gerbert, and Stephania, the widow of the murdered Roman Consul, Crescentius. The poem contains much fine work, and is picturesque and of poetical accent. . . ."—*Westminster Review*

ATTILA, MY ATTILA! A DRAMA IN FOUR ACTS. With a Facsimile of Two Medals. (Uniform with Stephania). Pott 4to. 5s. *net.*

"Attila, My Attila, is another of Michael Field's notable plays."—*Daily News.*

"Michael Field has already established a claim that what she writes should be read."—*Times.*

"A poetic drama, it is, for a wonder, poetry, and framed on no archaic pattern; its words speak to listeners of to-day."—*Album.*

GALTON (ARTHUR). TWO ESSAYS UPON MATTHEW ARNOLD, with his Letters to the Author. Fcap. 8vo. 3s. 6d. *net.*

"It is good to be reminded of the man himself, not only by the appearance of his delightful satire ('Friendship's Garland'), but by such books as this tiny volume."—*Times.*

"A small book, but more in it than n many a heavier appreciation of the great critic."—*Scotsman.*

GARLAND, ELKIN MATHEWS' SHILLING. A Series of Books of New Poetry by Various Authors, appearing at intervals. Cover design by SELWYN IMAGE. Fcap. 8vo. 1s. *net each part.*

NO. I. LONDON VISIONS. By LAURENCE BINYON.
[*Second Edition.*

GARLAND, SHILLING—*continued*.

"There seems to me to be no question at all about the uncommon worth of these poems. There are only twelve of them in all; others are going to appear later on . . . they are twelve genuine things cut out of the heart of London life, and some of them are poems of a big order. The stuff of poetry is in him, as it is in few of our pleasant verse-writers to-day; and I doubt if one of the London poets—I am not forgetting Mr. Henley—has put so much of actual London into his poetry, or looked at London sights more individually. . . . I have quoted much from a very little book, and I should like to quote more; but the rare pleasure of reading twelve poems by a new poet, not one of which is a mere experiment in rhythm, or follows any peculiar fashion of the day in thought or sentiment, leads one on to tempt others to share it. I hope Mr. Binyon has 'London Visions' enough to fill a great many more of Mr. Mathew's 'Shilling Garlands.'"—O. O., in *The Sketch*.

No. 2. PURCELL COMMEMORATION ODE, AND OTHER POEMS. By ROBERT BRIDGES. [*Second Edition.*

No. 3. CHRIST IN HADES, AND OTHER POEMS. By STEPHEN PHILLIPS, Author of "Eremus."

THE GARLAND, Volume I. (including "Christ in Hades") is now ready. The Shilling Edition of "Christ in Hades" is sold out, and can only be had in the bound volume.

"It is a wonderful dream, a dream that stirs the heart in almost every line, though Christ himself never utters a word throughout the poem, but only brings his sad countenance and bleeding brow and torn hands into that imaginary world of half conceived and chaotic gloom."—*Spectator*.

"The solemn music is matched by majestic words. The poignancy of feeling which is in the title-poem cries from the lyrics also."—*Speaker*.

No. 4. AËROMANCY, AND OTHER POEMS. By MARGARET L. WOODS. [*Second Edition.*

"'Aëromancy' is a fine poem, but there are others in the slim volume likely to be more popular; 'The Mariner's Sleep by the Sea,' for instance, and still more so, 'The Child Alone'—the latter a delightful picture of an imaginative child."—*Sketch*.

"It ['Aëromancy'] contains some very beautiful verses, but to the uninitiated reader they are somewhat incoherent. . . . The gems of the small selection are—'An April Song' and 'The Child Alone.' The former is the very life and breath of April at its best. . . . The latter is an exquisite sketch. . . . It would be impossible to express the elaborate and buoyant make-believe of an imaginative child's reverie with more force and humour than are given in these spirited verses."—*Spectator*.

No. 5. SONGS AND ODES. By Canon R. W. DIXON, Author of "Mano." Selected by ROBERT BRIDGES.

"The Odes have a sonorous stateliness and a warmth of colour which not infrequently reminds us of great masters."—*Speaker*.

SHILLING GARLAND—continued.

No. 6. THE PRAISE OF LIFE. By LAURENCE BINYON.
[*Second Edition.*

"Mr. Binyon is one of the most genuine and interesting of the younger poets. He is not facile, not popular, and he may never learn to be either. But he is one of those about whom you never ask why he writes poetry. As a craftsman, he is worth study. He makes interesting and often successful experiments in metre."—*Sketch.*

No. 7. FANCY'S GUERDON. By ANODOS, Author of "Fancy's Following."

"Certainly there is stuff of the true sort here. . . . Strange and impressive is the 'Day Dream,' truly like a dream is the bright exactness of its images, with its fine conclusion."—*Saturday Review.*

No. 8. ADMIRALS ALL, AND OTHER VERSES. By HENRY NEWBOLT.
[*Seventh Thousand.*

"Genuinely inspired patriotic verse. . . . There are but a dozen pieces in this shillingsworth, but there is no dross among them."—*St. James's Gazette.*

"All the pieces are instinct with the national English spirit. They are written in a sturdy rhythmical speech, worthy of their high themes."—*Scotsman.*

"Looking back to recent achievements in the same line, and including even Mr. Kipling's, we do not know where to find anything better after its own kind than his ballad of 'Drake's Drum.'"—*Westminster Gazette.*

"To the band of modern ballad-writers a new recruit is always most welcome. It is therefore with the greatest possible pleasure that we notice the delightful little collection of ballads which Mr. Newbolt publishes under the title of 'Admirals All.' Mr. Newbolt has done a notable thing. He has managed to write ballads full of ring and go, and full also of patriotic feeling, without imitating Mr. Rudyard Kipling. . . . 'Admirals All' is practically Mr. Stevenson's charming essay on 'The Old Admirals' put into ballad form. Mr. Newbolt has improved on the essay, and given us a poem which could be sung by sailors all the world over."—*Spectator.*

"Stirring ballads, written by a man who has force and spirit."—*Times.*

"These splendid songs will take an eminent and enduring place among our patriotic poetry."—*Daily Chronicle.*

"There are here all the qualities of ballad poetry, simplicity, directness, and vivid impression, and the quick sympathy which leaps from word to eye, and makes every reader yearn to be up and doing."—*Literature.*

"We should like to see these stirring verses in the hands of every high-spirited youth in the Empire.—*Globe.*

No. 9. INDIAN ELEGIES AND LOVE SONGS. By MANMOHAN GHOSE.

No. 10. SECOND BOOK OF LONDON VISIONS. By LAURENCE BINYON.

GARLAND, ELKIN MATHEWS'. Now Ready. Volume I., containing the first five numbers of above, with General Title, Contents, and Wrappers, bound in Cloth, gilt tops. 6s. *net.*

*_** After the issue of No. 10 of the "Shilling Garland," Volume 2 of "THE GARLAND" will be published uniform with and same price as above. See also note at end with regard to future Volumes.

GASKIN (ARTHUR). GOOD KING WENCESLAS. A Carol written by Dr. NEALE and Pictured by ARTHUR J. GASKIN; with an Introduction by WILLIAM MORRIS. 4to. 2s. 6d.
Transferred to the present Publisher.

GASKIN (MRS). DIVINE AND MORAL SONGS. By ISAAC WATTS. Fourteen Pictures in Colours, by Mrs. ARTHUR GASKIN, Printed by EDMUND EVANS. 16mo. fancy boards. 3s. 6d. *net.* [*Second Thousand.*

"A dainty little edition of Dr. Watts's 'Divine and Moral Songs.' ... The pages are rubricated, and the illustrations are exquisite in colour and pleasing in style."—*Glasgow Herald.*

"We have rarely, if ever, come across such a dainty and delicate edition of this old and popular children's favourite. Mrs. Gaskin's designs have a unique charm and a quaint originality which makes them positively delightful."—*Bookseller.*

A. B. C. An Alphabet Written and Pictured by MRS. ARTHUR GASKIN. 60 designs. Fcap. 8vo. 3s. 6d. *net.*
[*Second Thousand.*

"Quite an artistic book for children: the little rhymes to each letter are amusing, and the woodcut elaboration of each are of the dear old-fashioned sort that are always so charming."—*Glasgow Herald.*

GHOSE (MANMOHAN). *See* THE GARLAND.

GILLIAT-SMITH (ERNEST). FANTASIES FROM DREAMLAND (SAINT DUNSTAN'S DREAM,—A LEGEND FOR THE LITTLE ONES). With Cover Design and Illustrations by FLORI VAN ACKER. Crown 4to. 4s.

The accomplished Translator of "The Songs from Prudentius" in this volume deals with two delightful legends in the life of the Glastonbury Saint.

HAKE (DR. T. GORDON, "The Parable Poet"), MADELINE, AND OTHER POEMS. Crown 8vo. 5s. *net.*
Transferred to the present Publisher.

"I have been reading 'Madeline' again. For sheer originality, both of conception and of treatment, I consider that it stands alone."—MR. THEODORE WATTS-DUNTON.

HAKE (DR. T. GORDON)—*continued.*
PARABLES AND TALES. (Mother and Child.—The Cripple.—The Blind Boy.—Old Morality.—Old Souls.—The Lily of the Valley.—The Deadly Nightshade.—The Poet). With a Biographical Sketch by THEODORE WATTS-DUNTON. 9 illustrations by ARTHUR HUGHES. New Edition. Crown 8vo. 3s. 6d. net. [*In preparation.*

"The qualities of Dr. Gordon Hake's work were from the first fully admitted and warmly praised by one of the greatest of contemporary poets, who was also a critic of exceptional acuteness—Rossetti. Indeed, the only two review articles which Rossetti ever wrote were written on two of Dr. Hake's books: 'Madeline,' which he reviewed in the *Academy* in 1871, and 'Parables and Tales,' which he reviewed in the *Fortnightly* in 1873. Many eminent critics have expressed a decided preference for 'Parables and Tales' to Dr. Hake's other works, and it had the advantage of being enriched with the admirable illustrations of Arthur Hughes."—*Saturday Review.*

HALLAM (A. H.), THE POEMS OF, together with his Essay "ON SOME OF THE CHARACTERISTICS OF MODERN POETRY, AND ON THE LYRICAL POEMS OF ALFRED TENNYSON," reprinted from the *Englishman's Magazine*, 1831, edited, with an introduction, by RICHARD LE GALLIENNE. Small 8vo. 5s. *net.*

NEW BOOK ON CHARLES AND MARY LAMB.

HAZLITT (W. C.) THE LAMBS: THEIR LIVES, THEIR FRIENDS, AND THEIR CORRESPONDENCE. New Particulars and New Material. Thick crown 8vo. 6s. *net.*
[*Second Edition.*

This work contains (1) new biographical and bibliographical matter relative to Charles Lamb and his Sister; (2) sixty-four uncollected letters and notes from the Lambs, several of which have not hitherto been printed; and (3) certain letters to Lamb now first rendered.

"This interesting volume, the work of an enthusiastic Lambite, does contain some fresh matter . . . and will be seized upon with avidity by true Lamb-lovers . . . must needs place this volume on their shelves."—*Globe.*

"Contains some hitherto uncollected poems by Lamb, one of them simply a perfect specimen of playful album verse, and a great many valuable biographical particulars."—*Literary World.*

HEMINGWAY (P.). THE HAPPY WANDERER (Poems). Printed at the CHISWICK PRESS, on hand-made paper. Sq. 16mo. 5s. *net.*
Chicago: Way & Williams.

HEMINGWAY (P.)—*continued.*

"'The Happy Wanderer' is an exquisite volume where thought and expression alike are admirable. It should be read by all who are interested in the poetry of the day."—*Black and White.*

"Mr. Hemingway is thoughtful, and his felicity of phrase is more than occasional. His description of the sea as 'that mighty organ only God can play,' is very fine, and some of the sonnets—notably that which gives the title—linger in the memory and may not be forgotten."—*Review of Reviews.*

HINKSON (KATHARINE). A LOVER'S BREAST-KNOT: Lyrics by KATHARINE TYNAN (MRS. HINKSON). Decorated title-page. Fcap. 8vo. 3s. 6d. *net.*

"'A Lover's Breast Knot' is the tenderest, most musical, most exquisite book of poems which Katharine Tynan has so far given to her admirers."—*Literary World.*

HINKSON (H. A.) *See* DUBLIN VERSES.

"HOBBY HORSE (THE)." AN ILLUSTRATED ART MISCELLANY. Edited by HERBERT P. HORNE. The Fourth Number of the New Series will shortly appear, after which MR. MATHEWS will publish all the numbers in a volume, price £1. 1s. *net.*

Boston: Copeland & Day.

HORNE (HERBERT P.). DIVERSI COLORES: Poems. Vignette, &c., designed by the Author. Printed at the CHISWICK PRESS. 250 copies. 16mo. 5s. *net.*

Transferred to the present Publisher.

"In these few poems Mr. Horne has set before a tasteless age, and an extravagant age, examples of poetry which, without fear or hesitation, we consider to be of true and pure beauty."—*Anti-Jacobin.*

HUGHES (ARTHUR). *See* HAKE.

IBBETT (W. J.). A WEST SUSSEX GARLAND. ("Antæus"). Fcap. 4to. 2s. 6d. *net.* Only 50 copies for sale.

"IK MARVEL." *See* MITCHELL.

IMAGE (SELWYN). POEMS AND CAROLS. Title design by H. P. HORNE. Printed on hand-made paper at the CHISWICK PRESS. 16mo. 5s. *net.*

IMAGE (SELWYN)—continued.

"No one else could have done it (*i.e.*, written 'Poems and Carols') in just this way, and the artist himself could have done it in no other way." "A remarkable impress of personality, and this personality of singular rarity and interest. Every piece is perfectly composed; the 'mental cartooning,' to use Rossetti's phrase, has been adequately done . . . an air of grave and homely order . . . a union of quaint and subtly simple homeliness, with a somewhat abstract severity. . . . It is a new thing, the revelation of a new poet. . . . Here is a book which may be trusted to outlive most contemporary literature."—*Saturday Review.*

"An intensely personal expression of a personality of singular charm, gravity, fancifulness, and interest; work which is alone among contemporary verse alike in regard to substance and to form . . . comes with more true novelty than any book of verse published in England for some years."—*Athenæum.*

ISHAM FACSIMILE REPRINTS. Nos. III. and IV.

Breton (Nicholas). NO WHIPPINGE, NOR TRIPPINGE, BUT A KINDE FRIENDLY SNIPPINGE. London, 1601. A Facsimile Reprint, with the original Borders to every page, with a Bibliographical Note by CHARLES EDMONDS. 200 copies, printed on hand-made paper at the CHISWICK PRESS. 12mo. 5s. *net.*

When Dr. A. B. Grosart collected Breton's Works a few years ago for his "Chertsey Worthies Library," he was forced to confess that certain of Breton's most coveted books were missing and absolutely unavailable. The semi-unique example under notice was one of these.

S[outhwell] (R[obert]). A FOVREFOVLD MEDITATION, OF THE FOURE LAST THINGS. COMPOSED IN A DIUINE POEME. By R. S. The author of S. Peter's complaint. London, 1606. A Facsimile Reprint, with a Bibliographical Note by CHARLES EDMONDS. 150 copies. Printed on hand-made paper at the CHISWICK PRESS. Roy. 16mo. 5s. *net.*

This fragment supplies the first sheet of a previously unknown poem by Robert Southwell, the Roman Catholic poet, whose religious fervour lends a pathetic beauty to everything that he wrote, and future editors of Southwell's works will find it necessary to give it close study. The whole of the Poem has been completed from two MS. copies, which differ in the number of Stanzas.

The semi-unique originals from which these facsimiles are taken were discovered in the autumn of 1867 by Mr. Charles Edmonds, in a disused lumber room at Lamport Hall, Northants, and lately sold by Sir Charles Isham to the Trustees of the British Museum. Nos. I. and II. of these reprints are out of print and very scarce.

JACOBI (C. T.). GESTA TYPOGRAPHICA: a Collection of Printers' Sayings and Doings. Uniform with "On the Making and Issuing of Books." Fcap. 8vo. 3s. 6d. net.
50 copies also on Japanese Paper.

JOHNSON (LIONEL). POEMS. With a title design and colophon by H. P. HORNE. Printed at the CHISWICK PRESS, on hand-made paper. Crown 8vo. 5s. net.

"Full of delicate fancy, and display much lyrical grace and felicity."—*Times*.

"An air of solidity, combined with something also of severity, is the first impression one receives from these pages. . . . The poems are more massive than most lyrics are; they aim at dignity and attain it. This is, we believe, the first book of verse that Mr. Johnson has published; and we would say, on a first reading, that for a first book it was remarkably mature. And so it is, in its accomplishment, its reserve of strength, its unfaltering style. . . . Whatever form his writing takes, it will be the expression of a rich mind, and a rare talent."—*Saturday Review*.

IRELAND; with other Poems. Uniform with "Poems." Crown 8vo. 5s. net.

"A high place amongst living poets must be assigned to Mr. Lionel Johnson. The best poems in the volume before us, in their strength, stateliness, and severe simplicity, resemble some of Tennyson's most finished work. . . . . His former volume of poems, as well as this, will convince all appreciative readers that he possesses the creative faculty in a very high degree."—*Irish Daily Independent*.

"Mr. Lionel Johnson is now a poet of established reputation. His poems regarded at first as the austere exercises of a ripe scholar, have now taken their proper place by reason of the real fire and imaginative fervour which underlie their technical excellence."—*Westminster Review*.

KING (PAULINE). ALIDA CRAIG: A Novel. With Illustrations. Fcap. 8vo. 3s. 6d.

"A healthy and pleasantly-written story of a fast-vanishing type. . . . . Miss King makes no attempt to eke out her talent with the would-be clevernesses of the short story school; her characters are amiable without being angelic, and her style is characterised by a simplicity sometimes rising to distinction. The 'girl-bachelor who gives her name to the volume is a charming creation."—*Academy*.

LAMB (CHARLES and MARY). *See* HAZLITT.

LONGFELLOW. THE SINGERS, by HENRY W. LONGFELLOW. With 9 Etchings by ARTHUR ROBERTSON, A.R.E. Printed by F. GOULDING. Fcap. 4to. 2s. 6d. net.

Also an *Edition de Luxe*, limited to 40 copies, the principal Etchings signed by the Etcher, and each copy numbered. 10s. 6d. net. [*Nearly all subscribed.*

MARSON (CHARLES L.). TURNPIKE TALES. With cover design by EDITH CALVERT. Cr. 8vo. 3s. 6d.

CONTENTS :—Mr. Lavender and his Legacy ; Wild Grapes ; Miss Pattie's Rheumatism ; The Bishop ; A Realist of the Oldest School ; Love in a Mist; Abdias of Babylon ; A Satellite of Saturn.

"These short stories strike us as being the work of a clever man with a fine feeling for the literary value of phrases and sentences, and with a delicate sense of the humour and pathos of life."—*Daily Chronicle.*
"Will stir the social conscience as well as capture the intellect of their readers."—*Church Times.*

MARSTON (P. B.). A LAST HARVEST: LYRICS AND SONNETS FROM THE BOOK OF LOVE. Edited, with Biographical Sketch, by LOUISE CHANDLER MOULTON. Post 8vo. 5s. net.

"Among the sonnets with which the volume concludes, there are some fine examples of a form of verse in which all competent authorities allow that Marston excelled. 'The Breadth and Beauty of the Spacious Night,' 'To All in Haven,' 'Friendship and Love,' 'Love's Deserted Palace'—these, to mention no others, have the 'high seriousness' which Matthew Arnold made the test of true poetry."—*Athenæum.*

MEYNELL (WILFRID). THE CHILD SET IN THE MIDST. By MODERN POETS. With Introduction by W. MEYNELL, and Facsimile of the MS. of the "Toys" by COVENTRY PATMORE. Royal 16mo. 3s. 6d. net.

MITCHELL (DR. D. G., "IK MARVEL"). ENGLISH LANDS AND LETTERS. By the Author of "Reveries of a Bachelor." Thick cr. 8vo. 4s. 6d. net.

"Dr. Mitchell—famous the world over as 'Ik Marvel'—has laid literature under a fresh obligation by this volume. . . . Its limpid and graceful style."—*Home Journal.*

MOORE (EDWARD, D.D.). *See* DANTE.

MORRIS (WILLIAM). *See* GASKIN.

MORRISON (G. E.). ALONZO QUIXANO, otherwise DON QUIXOTE : being a dramatization of the Novel of CERVANTES, and especially of those parts which he left unwritten. Cr. 8vo. 1s. net.

"This play, distinguished and full of fine qualities, is a brave attempt to enrich our poetic drama. . . . The reverence shown for Cervantes, the care to preserve intact the characteristics the Spanish master lingered over so humorously, yet so lovingly, have led Mr. Morrison to deserved and notable success."—*Academy.*

NEWBOLT (HENRY). THE ISLAND RACE (with which is incorporated "ADMIRALS ALL"). Crown 8vo. 5s. net.
Of the forty Poems in this volume, twelve appeared in "Admirals All."

MORDRED: A TRAGEDY. Imp. 16mo. 3s. 6d. net.
Transferred to the present Publisher.
See THE GARLAND.

NICHOLSON (CLAUD). THE JOY OF MY YOUTH. A Novel. Crown 8vo. 3s. 6d.

"There is very delicate work in 'The Joy of My Youth.' There is not much story in it, but reminiscences from the history of a sensitive man, peculiarly open to impressions and influences from without. It has a Breton background, and, indeed, there is nothing at all English about it . . . . Its style, its sentiment, its attitude, were all made in France. It has charm and subtlety, and the childhood portion, with the blithe imaginative pictures of a beautiful and irresponsible past, must captivate all readers who have time to linger in their reading."—*Sketch.*

"The delicate charm of this story is not realised until the reader has read more than two or three chapters. The first chapter is unintelligible until the book is finished, and then we see that the author has chosen to tell us of the end of his hero's life before he has told us of the beginning of it. . . . . Mr. Nicholson writes with rare sympathy for and appreciation of French life."—*Glasgow Herald.*

"The hero is a charming child from first to last. . . . . Too delicate, too cultivated, most will vote the book; but that judgment will ignore its intention, which is fulfilled almost without a flaw."—*Bookman.*

NOEL (HON. RODEN). MY SEA, and other posthumous Poems. With an Introduction by STANLEY ADDLESHAW. Cr. 8vo. 3s. 6d. net.

"The volume now published from the materials the Hon. Roden Noel left behind him will no way detract from his fame as a poet. We have here notes of the same music that give so sweet and subtle a charm to his best poetry."—*Glasgow Herald.*

"The 'Nature Poems' have lines of great beauty and vigour."—*Sketch.*

"Many of the poems in this slender volume are among the best, in our opinion, that he ever wrote."—*Commonwealth.*

"A volume of strong and pathetic interest."—MR. A. E. FLETCHER, in the *New Age.*

"Such poems as 'Wild Love on the Sea,' with its ringing rhythm and the tender melodious 'To a Comrade,' leave little to be desired."—*Pall Mall Gazette.*

SELECTED POEMS, from the Works of the HON. RODEN NOEL. With a Biographical and Critical Essay by PERCY ADDLESHAW. With Two Portraits. Crown 8vo. 4s. 6d. net.

"The chief value of this volume is, of course, the examples it presents of Noel's poems. They are very fine. But the volume has an additional charm in Mr. Addleshaw's admirable biographical sketch, and the two beautiful portraits, which enable one much better to understand the noble nature of the poet."—*Glasgow Herald.*

O'SULLIVAN (VINCENT). POEMS. With a title design by SELWYN IMAGE. Printed at the CHISWICK PRESS on hand-made paper. (Uniform with LIONEL JOHNSON'S POEMS). Sq. cr. 8vo. 5s. net.

PHILLIPS (STEPHEN). See THE GARLAND.

POWELL (F. YORK). See CORBIN.

PROBYN (MAY). PANSIES: A BOOK OF POEMS. With a title-page and cover design by MINNIE MATHEWS. Fcap. 8vo. 3s. 6d. net.

"Miss Probyn's new volume is a slim one, but rare in quality. She is no mere pretty verse maker; her spontaneity and originality are beyond question, and so far as colour and picturesqueness go, only Mr. Francis Thompson rivals her among the English Catholic poets of to-day."—*Sketch.*

"This too small book is a mine of the purest poetry, very holy, and very refined, and removed as far as possible from the tawdry or the common-place."—*Irish Monthly.*

PUNCH PAPERS. See BROWNE.

RADFORD (DOLLIE). A LIGHT LOAD: a Book of Songs. With numerous full-page drawings and initial letters by BEATRICE PARSONS. Small 8vo. 5s. net.

"No woman could write a sweeter verse than the dedicatory stanzas of Dollie Radford's 'A Light Load.'"—*Speaker.*

"Of one piece, it should be said that it breathes the spirit of Mr. R. L. Stevenson's 'A Child's Garden of Verses.' Indeed there is not a song in this slender volume that would not bear quoting as an example of what a lyric should be."—*Daily Chronicle.*

"The songs are full of instinctive music which soars naturally. They have the choice unsought felicity of a nature essentially lyrical."—*Academy.*

"There is a song to quote on every page, and we must desist, but we are much mistaken if Mrs. Radford is not the possessor of a very rare and exquisite lyric gift indeed."—MR. RICHARD LE GALLIENNE, in the *Star.*

"Miss Parson's illustrations are all quite in harmony with the poems, and we could almost fancy that poet and artist had sat down together while the poems were being written and illustrated."—*Bookseller's Review.*

RHYMERS' CLUB, THE SECOND BOOK OF THE. Contributions by E. DOWSON, E. J. ELLIS, G. A. GREENE, A. HILLIER, LIONEL JOHNSON, RICHARD LE GALLIENNE, VICTOR PLARR, E. RADFORD, E. RHYS, T. W. ROLLESTONE, ARTHUR SYMONS, J. TODHUNTER, W. B. YEATS. 16mo. 5s. net. 50 copies on hand-made L.P. 10s. 6d. net.

RHYMERS' CLUB—*continued.*

"The work of twelve very competent verse writers, many of them not unknown to fame. This form of publication is not a new departure exactly, but it is a recurrence to the excellent fashion of the Elizabethan age, when 'England's Helicon,' Davison's 'Poetical Rhapsody,' and 'Phœnix Nest,' with scores of other collections, contained the best songs of the best song-writers of that tuneful epoch."—*Black and White.*

"The future of these thirteen writers, who have thus banded themselves together, will be watched with interest. Already there is fulfilment in their work, and there is much promise."—*Speaker.*

"In the intervals of Welsh rarebit and stout provided for them at the 'Cheshire Cheese,' in Fleet Street, the members of the Rhymers' Club have produced some very pretty poems, which Mr. Elkin Mathews has issued in his notoriously dainty manner."—*Pall Mall Gazette.*

ROSEN (LEW). NAPOLEON'S OPERA-GLASS : A HISTRIONIC STUDY. Crown 8vo. 3s. 6d. net.

"In this delightful little book Mr Rosen has performed a double task. He has collected for us, out of the first-hand authorities, anecdotes and sayings of Napoleon in regard to actors, acting, and dramatic literature, and he shows us how great and how conscious an actor Napoleon himself was when he himself took the stage on the theatre of life, and played some leading part."—*The Spectator.*

"The account of Napoleon's censorship of the stage makes very amusing reading. In fact, the whole book is decidedly interesting."—*Daily Mail.*

RUDING (WALTER). AN EVIL MOTHERHOOD. An Impressionist Novel. With a Frontispiece by AUBREY BEARDSLEY. Crown 8vo. 3s. 6d.

"The story is, indeed, a powerful one; a tale of wrong and suffering told in a vivid and thrilling language. It is in very truth the tragedy of a brain—its revolt, its suffering, its final passionate cries against the cruel wrong which sapped its strength, tortured its intellect and intelligence, and then left it thus shattered to fight the healthy world as best it could."—*Sunday Times.*

SARGANT (ALICE). *See* BALLADS.

SCHAFF (DR. PHILLIP). DANTE PAPERS. With Illustrations by W. T. HORTON. [*In preparation.*
LITERATURE AND POETRY. Engravings. 8vo. 10s. net.

SCULL (W. DELAPLAINE). BAD LADY BETTY : a Drama in Three Acts. Post 8vo. 1s. net.

"This clever and powerful play scarcely comes within our range. It gives, however, an animated picture of Lady Elizabeth Luttrell, the sister of the Duchess of Cumberland, and of other Luttrells of Four Oaks. It may be read with pleasure and interest, and, though not actable in its present shape, might perhaps be rendered so."—*Notes and Queries.*

SCULL (W. DELAPLAINE)—*continued.*
THE GARDEN OF THE MATCHBOXES, and other Stories. Crown 8vo. 3s. 6d.

"The author of these clever and fascinating fantasies is entirely abreast of the newest critical orthodoxy. . . . As literary craftsmanship, these maiden stories attain an unusually high and even level. They are all style. The variety of subject and motive is remarkable. As a whole, I take it, these tales mark the advent of a new story-teller, adequately equipped for the delineation of character, and possessed of acute psychological insight. Besides which, he can write.'—MR. GRANT ALLEN, in *Academy*.

"The beauty and pathos of 'A Certain Mr. Smith' will reward everyone for taking up the book."—*Manchester Guardian.*

"It is some time since we came upon more original work than this."—*Illustrated London News.*

SHARP (WILLIAM). ECCE PUELLA, AND OTHER PROSE IMAGININGS. Cr. 8vo. 3s. 6d. net.

"The book, as a whole, will appeal to all who have a keen palate for the more subtle flavours of literature."—*New Age.*

"Written in Mr. Sharp's brightest and happiest style."—*Leeds Mercury.*

SHILLING GARLAND (ELKIN MATHEWS'). *See* THE GARLAND.

SOME WELSH CHILDREN. By the Author of "Fraternity." With cover and title-page designed by the Author. Post 8vo. 3s. 6d.

Impressionist studies of child life in Wales, and intended to do for the Principality what "The Golden Age" has done for the Saxon Edward and Harold and Selina. The studies attempt to give the real character of the people, not as it is usually conceived, but as Rénan, with the fine intuition of kinship, divined it—the character of a people at once reserved and expansive, profoundly melancholy and childishly gay, independent and gentle, proud and timid—above all a nation of dreamers, whose dreams stretch back into the furthest reaches of antiquity.

SPAIN (IDYLLS OF). *See* THIRLMERE.

SPANISH ARMADA. A LETTER written on October 4, 1589, by Captain Cuellar, of the Spanish Armada, to H.M. King Philip II., recounting his Misadventures in Ireland and elsewhere after the Wreck of his Ship. Translated with Notes, by HENRY D. SEDGWICK. Finely printed on deckle-edge paper. 250 copies only. Fcap. 8vo. 2s. 6d. net.

STOW (ADA). *See* BABY LAYS, *and* MORE BABY LAYS.

STRANG (WILLIAM). *See* BALLADS.

SYMONDS (JOHN ADDINGTON). IN THE KEY OF BLUE, AND OTHER PROSE ESSAYS. With cover designed by C. S. RICKETTS. Printed at the BALLANTYNE PRESS. Thick cr. 8vo. 8s. 6d. *net.*
[*Third Edition.*
New York: Macmillan & Co.

"The variety of Mr. Symonds' interests! Here are criticisms upon the Venetian Tiepolo, upon M. Zola, upon Mediæval Norman Songs, upon Elizabethan lyrics, upon Plato's and Dante's ideals of love; and not a sign anywhere, except may be in the last, that he has more concern for, or knowledge of, one theme than another. Add to these artistic themes the delightful records of English or Italian scenes, with their rich beauties of nature or of art, and the human passions that inform them. How joyous a sense of great possessions won at no man's hurt or loss must such a man retain."—*Daily Chronicle.*

"The other essays are the work of a sound and sensible critic."—*National Observer.*

"The literary essays are more restrained, and the prepared student will find them ull of illumination and charm, while the descriptive papers have the attractiveness which Mr. Symonds always gives to work in this *genre.*"—MR. JAS. ASHCROFT NOBLE, in *The Literary World.*

TENNYSON (LORD). *See* HALLAM,—VAN DYKE.

THIRLMERE (ROWLAND). IDYLLS OF SPAIN. Varnished Pictures of Travel in the Peninsula. Cr. 8vo. 4s. 6d. *net.*

"An amusing book of travel. . . . The outcome of an exact observer's wanderings in Zaragoza, Barcelona, and other districts. They are less technically typographical than humorously human. They are brightly written, and thoroughly enjoyable."—*Daily Mail.*

"A bright, gossipy volume. . . . Some passages are perfect prose poems, and make the reader long for the fragrant breezes of the peninsula."—*Publisher's Circular*

"The book has roused many a pang of Reiselust."—*Bookman.*

"Here we have quality . . . The author apologises for his little book needlessly. He is a good traveller—a better impressionist. That indescribable charm of Northern Spain, of its inns, its people, and its romance, is one he can impart to us with signal success. There is here, too, that flutter of the petticoat without which, as Stevenson told us, even the strong book may fail to prove its strength. His meeting with little Marguerita is a subtle and very sweet sketch. He sought out remote inns: wherever romance was busy, there was his pen busy also. . . . It is an enjoyable journey; and we put down his volume with the thought that if all who write books of travel were as well equipped, life's way would be easier."—*Daily Chronicle.*

TYNAN (KATHARINE). *See* HINKSON.

VAN DYKE (HENRY). THE POETRY OF TENNYSON. Seventh Edition, enlarged. Cr. 8vo. 5s. 6d. net.

The additions consist of a Portrait, Two Chapters, and the Bibliography expanded. The Laureate himself gave valuable aid in correcting various details.

"Mr. Elkin Mathews publishes a new edition, revised and enlarged, of that excellent work, 'The Poetry of Tennyson,' by Henry Van Dyke. The additions are considerable. It is extremely interesting to go over the bibliographical notes to see the contemptuous or, at best, contemptuously patronising tone of the reviewers in the early thirties gradually turning to civility, to a loud chorus of applause."—*Anti-Jacobin*.

". "Considered as an aid to the study of the Laureate, this labour of love merits warm commendation. Its grouping of the poems, its bibliography and chronologys its catalogue of Biblical allusion and quotations, are each and all substantial accessorie, to the knowledge of the author."—DR. RICHARD GARNETT, in the *Illustrated London News*.

WATSON (E. H. LACON). AN ATTIC IN BOHEMIA: A Diary Without Dates. Crown 8vo. 3s. 6d.

"Mr. Watson discourses with shrewdness and humour upon such topics as diaries, tea and muffins, golf and matrimony. . . . There are 'ew writers who can treat so deftly and so entertainingly the most commonplace feelings and incidents of everyday life."—*Scotsman*.

"Another pleasant budget of essays is entitled 'An Attic in Bohemia,' by Mr. Lacon Watson. Mr. Watson preaches the comfortable doctrine of the desirability of loafing without being idle, and discourses with genuine humour and some philosophy. If the subject-matter is the obvious, the style is singularly fresh and graceful; it is always easy, without losing a pleasant literary flavour and without degenerating into slipshod slanginess. His humour is spontaneous (or seems to be so, because he has the art of concealing his art), and a trifle subacid at times, whereby it loses nothing in piquancy Of the seventeen essays which make up this little volume, there is not one which does not contain some happy fancy, some quaint conceit, or some shrewd reflection."—*Pall Mall Gazette*.

" If there are still any who, in the present epidemic of fiction, have any time to devote to that most delightful form of literature—the essay, let them order Mr. Watson's volume from their bookseller; for Mr. Watson has the rare talent of writing charmingly about nothing at all, and his essays are a delicate exposition of the triumph of spirit over ma'ter—which is, after all, the crowning achievement of pure literature. . . . Books like this make one realise regretfully how much most of us miss in our daily life for lack of the observant eye. . . . We hope Mr. Watson will give us some more of these charming 'causeries' before long.'—*Manchester Guardian*.

THE UNCONSCIOUS HUMOURIST, AND OTHER ESSAYS. Crown 8vo. 4s. 6d. net. [*Second Edition*.

" 'The Unconscious Humourist' is the title of the first essay in the book, but the subjects are as varied as 'Bicycle Tours—and a Moral,' 'The Literature of Reminiscence,' 'Confidences,' 'The Specialist,' ' On Love,' and 'Cacoethes Scribendi.' "

"These papers display a high and well-maintained standard of literary capacity, . . . Keenly introspective. . . Agreeably free from the cheap cynicism that characterises so many productions of this class."—*Daily Telegraph*.

WATTS-DUNTON (THEODORE). *See* HAKE.

WATTS (DR. ISAAC). *See* GASKIN.

[*Mr. Wedmore's Short Stories. New and Uniform Issue. Crown 8vo., each Volume 3s. 6d.*]

WEDMORE (FREDERICK). PASTORALS OF FRANCE. Fourth Edition. Crown 8vo. [*Sold out.*

"A writer in whom delicacy of literary touch is united with an almost disembodied fineness of sentiment."—*Athenæum*.
"Of singular quaintness and beauty."—*Contemporary Review*.

RENUNCIATIONS. Third Edition. With a Portrait by J. J. SHANNON. Cr. 8vo. 3s. 6d.

"These are clever studies in polite realism."—*Athenæum*.
"They are quite unusual. The picture of Richard Pelse, with his one moment of romance, is exquisite."—*St. James's Gazette*.
"'The Chemist in the Suburbs,' in 'Renunciations,' is a pure joy. . . . The story of Richard Pelse's life is told with a power not unworthy of the now disabled hand that drew for us the lonely old age of M. Parent."—MR. TRAILL, in *The New Review*.
"The book belongs to the highest order of imaginative work. 'Renunciations' are studies from the life—pictures which make plain to us some of the innermost workings of the heart."—*Academy*.
"Mr. Wedmore has gained for himself an enviable reputation. His style has distinction, has form. He has the poet's secret how to bring out the beauty of common things. . . . 'The Chemist in the Suburbs,' in 'Renunciations,' is his masterpiece."—*Saturday Review*.

ENGLISH EPISODES. Second Edition. Cr. 8vo. 3s. 6d. [*Very few remain.*

"Distinction is the characteristic of Mr. Wedmore's manner. These things remain on the mind as things seen; not read of."—*Daily News*.
"A penetrating insight, a fine pathos. Mr. Wedmore is a peculiarly fine and sane and carefully deliberate artist."—*Westminster Gazette*.

There may also be had the Collected Edition (1893) of "Pastorals of France" and "Renunciations," with Title-page by John Fulleylove, R.I. 5s. net.

WICKSTEED (P. H.). DANTE : SIX SERMONS. (Unaltered Reprint). Cr. 8vo. 2s. *net*. [*Fourth Edition.*

"It is impossible not to be struck with the reality and earnestness with which Mr. Wicksteed seeks to do justice to what are the supreme elements of the *Commedia*, its spiritual significance, and the depth and insight of its moral teaching."—*Guardian*.
"The book is one to be read slowly, carefully, lovingly; and those who do not feel when they come to the last page, that their time has been not only pleasantly but profitably spent, must choose for their amusement such literature as fits their need."—*Lady's Pictorial*.

WINSER (LILIAN). LAYS AND LEGENDS OF THE WEALD OF KENT, AS SUNG AND RECOUNTED AT A TWELFTH-NIGHT PARTY. With Illustrations by MARGARET WINSER. Crown 8vo. 5s. net.

WOODS (MRS. MARGARET L.). See THE GARLAND.

WYNNE (FRANCES). WHISPER! A Volume of Verse. Portrait. Fcap. 8vo. buckram. 2s. 6d. net.
Transferred by the Author to the present Publisher.

"A little volume of singularly sweet and graceful poems, hardly one of which can be read by any lover of poetry without definite pleasure, and everyone who reads either of them without is, we venture to say, unable to appreciate that play of light and shadow on the heart of man which is of the very essence of poetry." — *Spectator.*

"The book includes, to my humble taste, many very charming pieces, musical, simple, straightforward, and *not* 'as sad as night.' It is long since I have read a more agreeable volume of verse, successful up to the measure of its aims and ambitions."— MR. ANDREW LANG, in *Longman's Magazine.*

YEATS (W. B.). THE WIND AMONG THE REEDS (Poems). With a Portrait and Cover Design by Althea Gyles. Crown 8vo. 3s. 6d. net.

NOTICE.

The "Shilling Garland" will be suspended for a time, and (not necessarily superseding it) THE GARLAND of NEW POETRY: an Anthology of unpublished pieces by various Writers, will be issued ANNUALLY *in the Autumn.*

THE GARLAND OF NEW POETRY. With a Cover Design by LAURENCE BINYON. Fcap. 8vo. 3s. 6d. net.

LONDON: VIGO STREET, W.

www.ingramcontent.com/pod-product-compliance
Lightning Source LLC
Chambersburg PA
CBHW030335170426
43202CB00010B/1130